To:

....

From:

....

Date:

....

Praise for
The Better Mom Devotional

Whether your role as a mom finds you snuggling babies, chasing toddlers, helping a child with homework, or navigating the sometimes-trying teenage years, this encouraging devotional will help you to connect your heart straight to God's through the scriptures presented and the insight given. So step over the laundry, ignore the dirty dishes a little longer, and carve out a slice of time each day to meet with Jesus on the pages of this helpful and hopeful resource.

—KAREN EHMAN, Proverbs 31 Ministries speaker and *New York Times* bestselling author of *Keep It Shut: What to Say, How to Say It, and When to Say Nothing at All* and *Listen, Love, Repeat: Other-Centered Living in a Self-Centered World*, wife and mother of three

What mom doesn't need the life-breathing encouragement found in this beautiful devotional by Ruth Schwenk? She offers a short, but oh-so-sweet word for each day to give that godly perspective that we all crave as moms. Practical, down-to-earth, and yet inspiring too! Definitely a drink of cool water in that sometimes-thirsty land of motherhood.

—LISA JACOBSON, Club31Women.com

Probably one of the most important survival tools for moms in the trenches is time in the Word—and encouragement. Ruth tackles both beautifully in this devotional. I love Ruth's heart for moms. You see it in her blog and here in these pages. She gets it. Mom-life is hard. Each of these 100 devotions touches on elements of life where moms often struggle and need a little inspiration. What an incredible resource and blessing for moms.

—KRISTI CLOVER, author, speaker, and host of the *Simply Joyful Podcast*

How I wish I had Ruth Schwenk's *The Better Mom Devotional* ten years ago when I first felt terribly alone in my mothering. She gets it. This book holds the daily mentoring I need to encourage and uplift me as I raise my four sons!

—AMBER LIA, bestselling author of *Triggers* and *Parenting Scripts*

Every mom needs to take time to pause and refresh her spirit. Ruth's *The Better Mom Devotional* is filled with scripture and short devotions that will encourage you to start a dialogue with God each day. No matter what your day with your children brings you, this is just the inspiration you will need.

—Sandra E. Maddox, founder and coordinator of
Treasured Moms Ministry at Saddleback Church,
author of *Tiffany and The Talking Frog*,
and blogger at TheArtofDomesticity.com

A mother's super strength comes from a close relationship with the living God. *The Better Mom Devotional* will help you tap into the unlimited resources of heaven. Read it and be encouraged in your high calling of motherhood.

—ARLENE PELLICANE, speaker and author of *Parents Rising* and *31 Days to Becoming a Happy Mom*

the better Mom

DEVOTIONAL

Shaping Our Hearts as We Shape Our Homes

100 DEVOTIONS

ruth schwenk

ZONDERVAN®

ZONDERVAN

The Better Mom Devotional

Copyright © 2018 Ruth Schwenk

Requests for information should be addressed to:
Zondervan, 3900 Sparks Dr., SE, Grand Rapids, MI 49546

ISBN 978-0-3100-9545-3

The author is represented by the literary agency of The Fedd Agency, Inc., P. O. Box 34173, Austin, Texas 78734.

Art direction: Adam Hill
Interior design: Lori Lynch

Printed in China

20 21 22 23 24 GRI 11 10 9 8 7 6 5 4

Contents

Introduction

Dear friend,

I wish we were sitting across the table from each other, face to face, sipping cups of my favorite coffee and sharing our hearts—the joys, the struggles, the fears, and, of course, the hopes of motherhood. My prayer is that this devotional will be the next best thing. It's one way I hope to spur you on, inspire you to keep going, and remind you that you are not alone. We are in this together!

It's hard to believe, but nearly seven years ago, TheBetterMom.com was born. Over the past several years, hundreds of thousands of moms have joined and journeyed together, learning and growing through our daily devotions and social media presence.

At the heart of TheBetterMom.com and this devotional is the message that Jesus calls us to live not a weary life, but a worthy life. It's my sincere hope and prayer that God uses this devotional to encourage your mama heart and meet you right where you are.

The good news is that there is more to being a mom than the

extremes of striving for perfection or simply embracing the mess. Just as God is using us as moms to shape our children, God is using our children and motherhood to shape *us*. It's okay to come as we are, but our calling is far too important for us to stay there!

So I invite you to discover all that God wants to do in you through the devotions that follow. The way to becoming a better mom starts not with what we are doing, but with who God is inviting us to become.

Many blessings,

Ruth

the better Mom

DEVOTIONAL

Let God Be God

"I am God, and there is no other; I am God, and there is none like me. I make known the end from the beginning, from ancient times, what is still to come. I say, 'My purpose will stand, and I will do all that I please.'"

—ISAIAH 46:9–10

Every mom I know sometimes feels as if she's blown it. *Am I too lenient? Am I too strict? What could I do to better protect, teach, or guide my child?* Our kids don't come with an owner's manual, and that's one reason parenting is hard work. When our children are young, being a mom is physically exhausting. But as our children grow, motherhood becomes far more emotionally exhausting.

Because we love our children and desire to see them mature and walk wisely in the world, we can beat ourselves up over our parenting. We can get weary. Feel overwhelmed. Question whether our kids' mistakes will affect their futures. This is why we need the reminder of this truth: God is God—and we are not.

There are countless places in the Bible where God declared He is God. Although that seems obvious, the frequency of these reminders suggests just how often we forget. Instead of trusting God, we try to be God. Bad idea! We might not come right out and say it, or we might not even realize it. In many ways, though, our actions can reveal our lack of trust in the God who is ultimately in control of our lives—and our children's lives.

Friend, let's choose to rest in God's promises and trust Him for the future. And let's be faithful to what He has called us to do today. Even when we feel as if we are failing as moms, God's purposes for us and for our children never will. Let God be God.

Father, I need Your grace. I know that I don't always parent the best way. I need You. I need Your wisdom, Your grace, and Your power. Remind me that even when I feel like I'm failing, You are faithful to accomplish all of Your purposes. Give me hope and joy today as I serve and trust You. In Jesus' name, amen.

- In what part of your life are you struggling to trust God?
- How can the faithfulness of God be an encouragement to you as a mom today?

Loving by Listening

Turn your ear to me, come quickly to my rescue; be
my rock of refuge, a strong fortress to save me.

—PSALM 31:2

I heard Sophia, my youngest daughter, yell, "Mom!" And then again, "Mooom!" Growing in volume, the third cry came as I was on my way to see what was going on: "Mooooooom!" As it turns out, she needed toilet paper. Thankfully, nothing life-threatening!

As moms, we hear a lot. We can't help it. We hear cries for help. We get questions about homework, going outside, permission to watch a show or go to a movie. We hear conflicts and arguments erupting between siblings. Hearing is something we can't help. Hearing just happens.

But listening is different. We have to *choose* to listen. We choose to stop what we're doing. We choose to put away anything that might be a distraction. We choose to look into our child's eyes. We choose to sit down and ask more questions, choose to truly understand our children's hearts.

This is, after all, how God is with us. He not only hears us, but He listens to us. "Turn your ear to me," the psalmist cried to God. One translation says, "Bow down Your ear to me" (NKJV). Imagine that! The King of kings, whom we should bow down to, actually bows down His ear to us. He listens with His full attention.

What a great reminder for us moms. We can't help hearing, but we must choose to listen. Observe yourself today: how are you doing at truly listening to your children? Make it your goal to do more than just hear them; really listen.

Father, thank You for being a King who bows down Your ear to listen to me. I praise You and thank You for the undivided attention You give me. Help me as a mom not only to hear my children, but also to truly listen to them. Help me love them by bending my ear toward them. In Jesus' name, amen.

- What is the biggest difference between hearing and listening?
- What makes listening challenging for you as a mom?

Guard Against Grumbling

Give thanks to the LORD, for he is good;
his love endures forever.
—PSALM 107:1

I felt it long before I expressed it: that slow simmer of frustration. My grumbling, which almost always starts out feeling like a deep growl, would soon begin. I wanted a clean kitchen, a little help, and some peace and quiet, and the irritation I was feeling turned into grumbling. And then I began to verbalize my complaints out loud to my husband and, of course, to God.

Are you a grumbler? Do you always find something wrong? Maybe the house is never clean enough or the kids are never quiet enough. This kind of grumbling reveals our blindness to our blessings. Our complaining shows how we fail to see all we have. And most serious of all, our grumbling and complaining are really accusations toward God that life is not going the way we want or the way we think it should.

Grumbling is dangerous not only to our hearts but also to our homes. A complaining spirit can fill the atmosphere with a thick fog that hangs over everyone. That's why I love the reminder from the psalmist that we are to "give thanks." Giving thanks is, after all, the best antidote to complaining. Giving thanks silences our grumbling as we remind ourselves of all we have and don't deserve. Giving thanks always leads to gratefulness, gratefulness to joy, and joy to praise.

That's the kind of heart I want to have. That's the kind of home I want to cultivate. Let's start today. Let's nurture a heart and home that are filled with praise as we give thanks for all we have and don't deserve.

Father, open my eyes to truly see and appreciate all that You have given me that I don't deserve. Please teach me to guard my heart from focusing on what I don't have or on what I think I need. Fill me with thankfulness. Help me find joy in You, thanking You for all that You have done, are doing, and will do. In Jesus' name, amen.

- In what ways can complaining be bad for your home?
- What can you begin to do today to cultivate a home characterized by gratitude instead of grumbling?

Don't Go It Alone

One who has unreliable friends soon comes to ruin,
but there is a friend who sticks closer than a brother.
—PROVERBS 18:24

We haven't only been saved into a relationship with Jesus; we've also been saved into a relationship with Jesus' people with God as our Father. Together we are growing up as God's family. Relationships were never meant to be optional in the Christian life.

Why does God put such an emphasis on relationships? Because they are one of the primary ways He works in us to teach us, encourage us, and grow us.

Sometimes, though, friendships get pushed to the back burner when kids come along. It's far easier for many of us to be private instead of vulnerable, busy instead of available, and isolated instead of interdependent. As a result, we miss out on the joy and blessing of sharing life with other friends. Yes, relationships take work, but the effort is so worthwhile.

At the very beginning of the Bible, God said it is not good for a man to be alone (Genesis 2:18). Together, the first man and woman would have the capacity for intimate love and meaningful friendship, both of which help show the world what God is like (Ephesians 5:21–27). The rest of the Bible shows us that life is meant to be lived in community with others.

One of the greatest dangers of motherhood is not just isolation from our spouses, but isolation from other people. We were meant to live in relationships with others who will encourage us, pray for us, listen to us, and even hold us accountable.

Do you need to make friendship more of a priority? Is there someone you need to seek out for wisdom, encouragement, or just companionship? Be careful of trying to be a mom on your own! You weren't meant to go it alone. Friends are an incredible gift. God uses relationships to help us become better not just at what we are doing, but also better at who we are becoming.

Lord, thank You for the gift of friends. Help me be more intentional about nurturing my friendships. Guide me to those women I should seek out to learn from and to those I can be a friend to. In Jesus' name, amen.

- What is the biggest obstacle keeping you from deeper friendships right now?
- Is there a friend or even an acquaintance you can encourage, pray for, or call today?

Hiding God's Word in Your Heart

I have hidden your word in my heart
that I might not sin against you.
—PSALM 119:11

If you ask my husband, he would tell you our closet could double as a store. Over the years I have accumulated a fair number of shoes, purses, scarves, and accessories. The truth is, I could live without them. There is something far more valuable the Bible tells us to treasure or store up.

In Psalm 119:11, the writer reminded us of the importance of storing and treasuring God's Word in our hearts. He has made room and stored up the most valuable resource there is—God's truth and promises.

We hide God's Word in our hearts as we read it, meditate on it, memorize it, cling to it, pray it, and sing it. We store it in our hearts because it gives us strength. It protects us. Sustains us. Convicts us. And it also is one of the primary ways God is making us better, more like Christ (Romans 12:2).

In the busyness and messiness of motherhood, it's easy to forget what is most important. We can let daily tasks get in the way of feeding on our daily bread. What our hearts need most is to be filled with what lasts. We need the power and truth of God's Word to keep us going and to guard us from sin.

What will you fill your heart with today? What will you treasure? What will you make room to store up? Whatever you do, make it a priority to hide God's Word in your heart!

Father, I believe that You are the God who speaks. You have made Yourself known to me through Your Word. Would You comfort me, strengthen me, convict me, and guide me as I store Your words in my heart? Give me ears to hear You and strength to obey You today. In Jesus' name, amen.

- In what ways do you need to hide God's Word right now?
- What is one verse or passage you can store in your heart today?

Showing Honor in Your Marriage

Be devoted to one another in love. Honor
one another above yourselves.
—ROMANS 12:10

I'll never forget walking down the aisle on our wedding day and seeing Patrick waiting for me. We walked into the church separately that day, but we took our first steps as a married couple as we walked out together. And walking down the aisle was the easiest part of walking through life together. Real challenges come, and that's why we need reminders to stay committed and be careful with each other as the years go by.

The Bible says we are to "be devoted to one another in love." We are to be prone to affection for, committed to, and holding fast to our spouses. And not only that, but we are to "honor one another," putting our spouses before ourselves. Sadly, we don't always cherish each other as we should.

Showing honor involves committing to respect each other. Being gentle with our words. Elevating, not degrading, each other. Seeking to protect our intimacy. Showing grace. And always fighting for and not against each other. We are to handle our spouses with care, treating our husbands as the gifts from God and the treasures they actually are. Honoring each other means using our differences, not to compete with one another, but to complement one another.

How are you honoring your husband? Do you cherish him with your words, attitude, and actions? Today, ask God to give you and your husband the heart to honor each other in your marriage. Ask for an increasing desire to do what is best for the other. Stick together. Be devoted. Honor and cherish each other just as God cherishes you!

Father, help me truly respect my husband. Help me watch my words, guard my heart, and be mindful of my actions. Holy Spirit, empower me to build up, not tear down, my husband. Help us to fight for, and not against, each other. May the love You have for us be the kind of love we express to each other. In Jesus' name, amen.

- What is the biggest obstacle to your showing honor to your husband?
- What is one way you can honor your husband? If you're not sure, ask him.

Say Goodbye to the Perfect Home

Share with the Lord's people who are
in need. Practice hospitality.
—ROMANS 12:13

When I heard the doorbell ring, I was immediately terrified. We were eating dinner as a family, so I quickly peeked out the window to see who was there. When I saw several friends who had stopped by unexpectedly, my heart sank. You see, my home was a complete mess, and I really didn't want them to see it that way.

"Come on in," I said sheepishly. Secretly, I was hoping they were just passing by and that a quick hello and goodbye would be enough. I was more than happy to see them, but not so thrilled at the thought of their seeing flustered me and my not-so-picture-perfect home. I had been gone all day. Laundry was piled in the family room. Toys littered the hallway. Dinner, along with its remnants, was clearly visible on—and under—the table.

But to my surprise, what started out with my uncomfortable invitation to come in turned into an important revelation for me. I discovered that my presence is far more important than the perfect home. What makes a home is not the brick and mortar or whether it's spotless or stylish. What makes a home is the presence of the people who live there.

For many years of being a mom, I was nervous about opening our home to others because I was afraid it wasn't big enough, and I certainly couldn't have it cleaned up enough. I mistakenly thought my home had to be perfect before I could practice hospitality.

Do you struggle to invite people to your house? Are you nervous about what someone might think of your home? Don't let your idea of perfection keep you from inviting people in. Remember that your presence is far more valuable to them than the perfect home.

Father, help me get over my fear of what others think about my home or about me. Instead, help me welcome others into my home and focus on being fully present with my guests. Teach me to open the door to the home You have given me so I can love, serve, and bless others. In Jesus' name, amen.

- In this messy mission of motherhood, how have you let your idea of perfection keep you from investing in other people?
- How can you begin to let go of your idea of the perfect home and invite others in?

Words Matter

Gold there is, and rubies in abundance, but lips
that speak knowledge are a rare jewel.

—PROVERBS 20:15

How would you describe the tone of your home? Is the atmosphere tense? Are people noisy or argumentative? Or is the tone peaceful and encouraging? The truth is, it's probably a combination of any or all of the above at different times!

Whether we like it or not, we moms are most often the ones who set the tone of the home. And our words are one of the primary ways we do that.

The Bible has a lot to say about our words. When God spoke in the beginning, His words brought life, light, and beauty. Just as God's words have power, so do ours. One way we reflect who God is to those around us is by our words.

Every day we can choose to use words that bring encouragement, truth, and hope. Or we can speak words that cause hurt, division, and confusion. As moms, we do more than just communicate information to our kids; the words we speak shape young hearts. So God wants us to be careful with how we wield the enormous power of our words.

The Bible also reminds us that our words reveal what is in our hearts. If a tree isn't producing fruit, the problem is in the root system. Our real struggle with words is actually a problem with our hearts.

What kind of tone are you setting in your home with your words? Are you speaking life, truth, and encouragement to those around you? Today, make a decision to do exactly that. Ask God to change your words by changing your heart.

Lord, You are a God who speaks. When You communicate, You do so with love, truth, and power. Help my words reflect who You are. Change me from the inside out. Use my words to bring life, joy, peace, and truth to my home. In Jesus' name, amen.

- What do your words most often reveal about your heart?
- How can you begin to change the tone of your home today by changing your words?

Expecting Progress, Not Perfection

Encourage the disheartened, help the
weak, be patient with everyone.
—1 THESSALONIANS 5:14

Are your expectations for your kids too high? Is the bar set so high that only Jesus could actually succeed?

It's okay to have high standards for our kids. We should call them to live up to all that God has for them and desires for them. But expecting too much, too soon, can be unhealthy for our kids and unhealthy for us as well. Instead, we should be patient, focusing on progress, not perfection.

Unrealistic expectations may leave our kids feeling deflated and defeated. Our desire for perfection teaches our kids that they are loved only when they are performing well. Just as we do, our kids are going to make mistakes. They're going to choose foolishly instead of wisely. At times they'll listen to our coaching or counsel, but many times they won't. Our kids are still in the process of growing up.

The Bible reminds us that there is a time to warn, challenge, encourage, help, instruct, and even discipline. Our goal is not just to raise good kids; our goal is to raise kids who will love Jesus and love the world. But this calling is not entirely ours. The same grace that saved us is the same grace that will grip our kids' hearts. It is God's goodness and not our great parenting that ultimately changes our kids' hearts. We have a part to play, for sure. But remaining patient with our kids allows us to do our part while trusting God to do His.

So keep loving and teaching your kids. Don't become complacent. Be realistic. Be patient. Remember who is at work in and through your parenting.

Father, thank You for being patient with me. Help me love and care for my kids in a way that is patient, kind, and wise. Remind me that perfection is found only in You. In Jesus' name, amen.

- Are there areas where you expect too much from your kids?
- How can you be more patient, focusing on progress instead of perfection?

Our Strong God

In the beginning God created the heavens and
the earth. Now the earth was formless and empty,
darkness was over the surface of the deep, and the
Spirit of God was hovering over the waters.

—GENESIS 1:1–2

From its first lines, the Bible tells us that we have a God who is the Almighty! He is not a pushover. He is clothed with strength and glory. That is what *Elohim*, the very first name of God in the Bible, means. The names of God throughout the Bible tell us something special about His character and His identity.

Genesis 1:1 tells us, "In the beginning God [*Elohim*] created the heavens and the earth." This name of God is used more than two thousand times in the Bible.[1] And guess how many times you'll find it in Genesis 1? Thirty-two times!

The Bible starts with God. He is our Creator and Sustainer. We are not alone in the world. God created us to be in relationship with Him and to live for Him. He is our strong and powerful heavenly Father. He is the

King who reigns and rules over all of His creation. He is our Protector and Provider.

Are you struggling to make it as a mom? Are you worried or anxious about the future? Remember, your powerful God is in charge. You and I are limited in our power and wisdom, but He is not. He is *Elohim*—the Almighty! There is nothing you are facing today that He cannot match with His presence and power.

Father, I praise You for Your strength and might. Nothing takes You by surprise. The world is not out of control. You are a good Father, but also a powerful King over all of creation. Help me trust You, relying on Your strength and not my own. In Jesus' name, amen.

- The first Hebrew name of God we find in the Old Testament is *Elohim*. What is significant about this name of God being used so many times in Genesis 1?
- For what aspect of parenting do you need to remember and rely on God's power, not your own?

the Hard places that Make Us Holy

Remember how the Lord your God led you all the way in
the wilderness these forty years, to humble and test you in
order to know what was in your heart. . . . He humbled you,
causing you to hunger and then feeding you with manna, . . .
to teach you that man does not live on bread alone but
on every word that comes from the mouth of the Lord.

—DEUTERONOMY 8:2–3

The word *holy* sounds intimidating, but it simply means to be set apart. When God commanded us to be holy, He means we are to be set apart from sin and set apart for Him. He loves us, pursues us, and saves us, and He desires to continue the work of setting us apart from sin. To say it another way, God wants each of us to grow up and become more mature—more like Christ.

One of the ways He does this work in us is through the hard places of life—and that includes parenting. In fact, God is using parenting to make us holy. God will often lead us to hard places to make us more like Him.

We'd all probably like to fast-forward through trials. Sometimes in the hard places it feels as if God is taking things away from us when He's actually giving us a good gift: He's teaching us to depend on Him. To trust Him. To rely on Him. He causes us to hunger and thirst for Him, but then He feeds us with what we need most. God gives us the gift of Himself.

The hardest places can often be the holiest places—the spaces where God does some of His greatest work. Will you let Him do the heart work even when it is in a hard place? Will you keep trusting Him, obeying Him, and seeking Him even when it is difficult?

Father, my greatest need is knowing and treasuring You. I want to surrender to You, not resist You. Fill me with Your Spirit and help me grow, becoming more holy, even when life is hard. In Jesus' name, amen.

- Why are hard places necessary for your growth and maturity?
- As you are raising your kids, how is God using motherhood to make you more like Christ?

Rooted in God's Love

We love because he first loved us.

—1 JOHN 4:19

As I get older I have come to appreciate more and more the true value of friendship. I can't imagine life without my dear friends who encourage me and challenge me in many ways. But as much as I love and cherish my friends, they were never meant to fill a void that only God can. A healthy friendship blossoms when two people first root themselves in God's love for them. Simply put, friendships are a beautiful gift but a terrible god.

As we seek to build and maintain God-honoring friendships during this busy season of motherhood, we need to be sure we're rooted in God's love. We do that by getting alone with God often. Spending time in His Word. Meditating on what He has done for us. Cherishing His promises. Receiving the love He longs to lavish on us. Allowing His acceptance and approval of us to ground us and grow us.

Why is being rooted in God's love so important in friendship? Because then we won't look to our friends for the kind of love and approval only

God can give us. Furthermore, the more we root our lives in God's love, the more freely we will be able to give our love to our friends.

So be a good friend. But most importantly, seek love from God first. Rest in His unconditional and unwavering approval. The more you receive and experience His love, the more you'll be able to give it to others!

Father, I want to know and experience the love You have for me in Christ. Help me rest in Your approval and acceptance. Help me trust that Your opinion of me never changes, and remind me that only You can completely satisfy me. You meet all of my needs. Pour out Your Spirit in my heart today so that I might love those around me. In Jesus' name, amen.

- What is one way you can look to God *first* for love, even before turning to a friend?
- How can you—as a godly friend—encourage your friend to also seek God first??

Learning to Pray

Jesus was praying in a certain place, and when
he finished, one of his disciples said to him, "Lord,
teach us to pray, as John taught his disciples."

—LUKE 11:1 ESV

*A*sking for help doesn't come easily to me. Just ask my husband! I'd rather try to figure it out, wrestle with a problem for a while, before I reach out in need. It's one thing to take this approach when you're trying to put together a new desk from IKEA and quite another when you're trying to shape souls. That's why in the messy and beautiful mission of parenthood, we need to ask for help. At its core, this is what prayer is all about.

We begin to pray when we come to the end of ourselves. We cry out to God as we realize that we aren't God. Lacking His wisdom, strength, and resources, we recognize our need for help. So we pray, and we pray often. It's something we all have to learn to do because it's much easier, if not more natural, to be self-sufficient—or at least to pretend we are.

I love that the disciples went to Jesus and said, "Teach us to pray." For years, I read that verse as if it said, "Teach us *how* to pray." Certainly, that was part of what Jesus' first followers were asking. But for so many of us moms, we need to learn *to* pray before we learn *how* to pray. The mission of being a mom is too big and too important for us to try to pull off on our own. We learn *how* to pray only after we discover that we *need* to pray.

As moms, we often feel helpless. On any given day, our children will encounter countless things that are completely out of our control. Our strength is limited. We won't always make the right decisions. And so we pray—because we need to.

God is big. He is wise. His love is infinite. Whatever you or your children are facing today, run to God. Don't try to carry those burdens on your own!

Father, thank You that You alone are wise, powerful, and loving. Help me lean on You, and remind me that I need to pray. Give me enough humility to know that I am helpless without You. In Jesus' name, amen.

- In what areas of your life do you need to be more dependent on God and less self-sufficient?
- What part of God's character do you need to be reminded of in order to trust Him as you raise your children?

Two Becoming One

A man leaves his father and mother and is united
to his wife, and they become one flesh.
—GENESIS 2:24

The oneness a man and a woman can experience in marriage is a beautiful and profound experience. A husband and wife share their love, hearts, bodies, emotions, dreams, struggles, successes, and more. But oneness never just happens. God gives us this gift of one another. He brings us together, but through His power, we have to work to stay together.

There is nothing more painful than a divided marriage, that heartbreaking sense of separation and distance. We can be divided, or remain "two," for a lot of reasons. Differences in personality, preferences, self-discipline, hobbies, or interests can drive a wedge between a husband and wife. But God created us to be united in our marriages; He wants us to know the oneness of marriage. He wants the two spouses to become one.

Even the first man and woman God brought together didn't stay one for long. As sin entered the garden of Eden, sin entered their marriage.

It contaminated the beauty of oneness. Their sin and selfishness pushed them away from God and from each other.

A strong and healthy marriage is growing in oneness, and we need to protect, nurture, and fight for that oneness. We can't just wait and hope for oneness to happen. We need to talk about it and work toward it. Be humble and ask God to grow you and your spouse in the areas of your marriage where you feel most divided.

Father, protect my marriage from being divided. I confess the ways my sin can separate us. Teach me to walk in humility. Show me where we need to be more united. And give us the power to set aside some of the differences that divide us. Lord, empower us to be one. Don't give the enemy a foothold. Don't allow him to get between my husband and me. In Jesus' name, amen.

- What is the one area in which you feel most divided in your marriage right now? What is one step you can take to move toward oneness in this area?
- How can you guard the oneness you do have with your spouse?

At Home with Purpose

As for me and my household, we will serve the LORD.
—JOSHUA 24:15

What is the purpose of your home? Beyond just living in your home, what are you trying to accomplish there for your family?

In Deuteronomy 6, we learn that the home is to be a central place for God's ways to be both taught and lived out. God loves the family. And it is His desire to see our home be a place where we are passing on faith to the next generation. He made this clear in Deuteronomy 6:

> These commandments that I give you today are to be on your hearts. Impress them on your children. Talk about them when you sit at home and when you walk along the road, when you lie down and when you get up. (vv. 6–7)

God's truth, love, and promises are to be in our hearts, but that doesn't happen simply by living under the same roof. That's why we are to "impress" God's truth on our kids. We are to talk about who God is and what He has done when we "sit at home." We are to be intentionally training and equipping our kids with faith on the way to school, around the dinner table, while we're sitting on the back deck, or while we're tucking them in at night. "When you lie down and when you get up," the Bible says, our homes should be places for God's presence to dwell and God's purposes to be fulfilled.

Take some time this week to consider how you can use your home more intentionally for a purpose. Write a mission statement that uniquely fits your family and home. Ask yourself, *How can we use our home to love and serve others?* Talk with your family about simple and practical ways you as a family can live for God's glory right where He has you.

Father, thank You for the gift of my family. Teach me to count my days so that I can make my days count. Give me strength and wisdom to live with greater purpose, loving, teaching, and equipping my kids to one day leave my home. In Jesus' name, amen.

- How would you currently describe the purpose of your home?
- What is one way you can begin living more on purpose as a family?

Not to Us

Not to us, Lord, not to us but to your name be the
glory, because of your love and faithfulness.
—PSALM 115:1

We were created to live for Someone bigger than ourselves. God fashioned us so that every part of who we are and what we do reflects who He is. He made us to live for His glory, not our own.

The psalmist wanted us to be sure we don't miss this truth. It wasn't enough for him to say it just once; he chose to say it twice: "Not to us, Lord, not to us." Our jobs. This calling. These circumstances. All of our unique gifts, experiences, and passions. Our current places in life. All of it is "not to us . . . not to us." But instead, all of it is to God and for God. "To your name be the glory, because of your love and faithfulness."

In a culture that values the individual and encourages each of us to make a name for ourselves, the gospel calls us to lose ourselves. To die to ourselves and live for God's greatness. Instead of pursuing our own fame, we are called to faithfulness. God wants each of us, no matter where we are, to faithfully bear witness to who He is and what He has done.

There is no greater joy than honoring and obeying Christ. Sometimes it's in big ways, but often it's in small, mundane, and even unnoticed ways. Only when we are living for His fame will we find lasting joy and satisfaction.

God has placed you where you are on purpose. Our faithfulness is the stage on which God performs, working in and through us for His glory. Who are you living for today?

Father, You have created me to live for You. It is Your name and Your name alone that is worthy of praise. Help me honor You and live for Your glory. Teach me to be faithful right where You have me, bearing fruit for Your kingdom. In Jesus' name, amen.

- How have you seen your own ambition become self-centered?
- What is one thing you can do today to be faithful right where God has you?

Mind Games

The mind governed by the flesh is death, but the
mind governed by the Spirit is life and peace.

—ROMANS 8:6

Does your mind control you, or do you control your mind? Does worry ever take you captive? What about fear? I know the infamous "what if" takes me hostage from time to time! Our minds are powerful, which is why if we don't control them, they will control us.

So what can we do to keep our thoughts from running wild? After all, what we think has a lot to do with the people we are becoming. It's no wonder the Bible has so much to say about our thoughts. For example, we are to have our minds renewed (Romans 12:2). We are to think about what is true, noble, right, pure, lovely, and admirable (Philippians 4:8). Now that we are in Christ, we are to put on a new attitude (Ephesians 4:23). But the power to change how we think doesn't come from us; rather, it comes from God's Spirit.

God gives us the gift of His Spirit to help us control our wandering minds that too often can war against our hearts. He gives us resources when our thoughts roam and turn into worry, fear, anxiety, or maybe even anger.

In Romans 8:6, we are told to allow God's Spirit to control our thinking. We are to surrender every thought to God's power and presence, letting Him remind us of His love, truth, and grace. When we let God's Spirit control and correct our thinking, we experience life and peace.

So don't let your thoughts control you. Let God's Spirit guard your heart and guide your thinking.

Father, I confess that my mind easily strays from Your truth. I know that my thoughts of worry and fear need to be controlled and corrected. I want to surrender my mind to You, allowing Your love, truth, and grace to guard my thoughts. Keep me from doubting and not trusting You. In Jesus' name, amen.

- According to the apostle Paul, what happens when you let your flesh instead of the Holy Spirit guide your thinking?
- What part of your thought life right now most needs to be controlled or corrected by God's Spirit?

Extend Your Family

To Timothy my true son in the faith: Grace, mercy and
peace from God the Father and Christ Jesus our Lord.
—1 TIMOTHY 1:2

We had just finished eating dinner when the doorbell rang. I had a
pretty good guess who it was. Sure enough, as I opened our front
door, I saw four kids from our neighborhood eagerly waiting for our children to be done with dinner.

Since we moved in to our new neighborhood, our home has become
the gathering place for basketball, capture the flag, football, and everything in between. I could feel the kids' disappointment when I said, "Our
kids can't come out yet. We're just finishing up dinner, and we're getting
ready to do our devotions."

That's when I felt God nudge me to invite them in. So I did. Before
I knew it, we were having not just family devotions; we were having
extended-family devotions. I realized that God was using us not only to
influence our kids, but to plant seeds of His life-changing truth in the
lives of their friends.

God has placed our children in our lives for a purpose, and through them He has placed other kids in our lives too. They might be kids in our neighborhood. Our kids' friends and classmates. Kids in our church. These children, while not our own biological children, can be children of ours "in the faith," just as Timothy was to Paul.

Timothy was a younger Christian and a pastor, and Paul described him as "my true son in the faith." The fact is, God's family is bigger than our own family by blood.

So prayerfully consider what influence you might have not only on your own kids, but also on the friends who come over to play, join you for dinner, or just hang out at your house. God wants to use your family to extend His.

Lord, Your family is so much bigger than just my own. Help me intentionally connect with my kids' friends and those friends' moms. Give me opportunities to influence them by speaking truth, encouraging them, praying for them, and loving them for Your glory. In Jesus' name, amen.

- Outside of your own family, which people were most influential in your faith while you were growing up?
- What are one or two things you can do to begin to extend your family?

Disciplining with Love

The LORD is compassionate and gracious, slow to anger,
abounding in love.... As a father has compassion on his
children, so the LORD has compassion on those who fear him.
—PSALM 103:8, 13

It doesn't take us moms very long to discover that our little bundles of joy are not perfect. As our children grow up and begin making decisions on their own, we quickly see them make choices that are not always right. So how do we respond when our kids disobey? How do we react when we know they have chosen unwisely? Do we discipline in love, or do we discipline by inducing guilt?

If you're reading this book, you undoubtedly want to lovingly discipline your children when they disobey, teach them what is right and what is wrong, and help them ask the Lord for the ability to do what pleases Him. Essential to disciplining in love is showing our kids that we still cherish them and accept them despite their sin. This is the heart of the gospel.

The danger of disciplining with guilt is that it is often rooted in anger. Angry parents tend to address the children's behavior and miss their hearts. Our children need to rightly understand the Holy Spirit's conviction. Sin is serious, and its consequences are real. But disciplining with guilt alone can leave a child living under the weight of condemnation. Why is this so dangerous?

Making our kids feel guilty communicates that acceptance and approval are based on their performance. The good news is good because we are saved not by our performance, but by the performance of Jesus. Because of Christ, the Father looks on us with acceptance and approval. We demonstrate the gospel to our children when we reaffirm our love for them even when they make mistakes (Romans 5:8).

So be careful not to express your love for your children only when they perform well. The next time they fail, be sure to let your kids know how much you still love them.

Father, help me love my kids with compassion, patience, instruction, and gentleness. Let Your love flow through me so that even when my kids misbehave or make mistakes, they know they are loved and accepted. In Jesus' name, amen.

- In what situations have you been tempted to discipline with guilt?
- What is one change you can make so that you more consistently discipline out of love?

the Surest Foundation

I love you, Lord, my strength. The Lord is my rock, my fortress
and my deliverer; my God is my rock, in whom I take refuge,
my shield and the horn of my salvation, my stronghold.
—PSALM 18:1–2

All of us are building our lives on something. We can build on our careers, a relationship, possessions, physical ability, or appearances. We can even build our lives around something as good as parenting. But what do we do when that foundation we've been building on begins to crack?

Maybe a relationship you thought was secure has fallen apart. Maybe motherhood is much more difficult than you imagined. Maybe your health that once seemed invincible is failing. Or your impeccable reputation has been undermined by falsehood. Where do you look when you discover that your foundation wasn't as strong as you thought it was?

Looking to God, the Rock, is the best alternative. But it's one thing to say God *is* a Rock and quite another to say God is *my* Rock.

To say that God is my Rock is to admit that we are weak. It's an acknowledgement that apart from Him we aren't good enough, brave enough, righteous enough, or faithful enough. When God is our Rock, we have a place to run to for refuge. We can lean on Him. We can stand on His love and His truth. He is the only foundation for our lives that is sure footing.

In the New Testament, Jesus echoed these words: "Everyone who hears these words of mine and puts them into practice is like a wise man who built his house on the rock" (Matthew 7:24). His life and words are the only foundation that will not give out. When we build our lives on Him, we can be confident that even though everything around us gives way, we are safe and secure in Him.

Father, thank You for being my Rock. You are my refuge. You are my hiding place—the One who fights for me, protects me, and keeps me secure when all else fades away. Draw near to me today as I draw near to You. In Jesus' name, amen.

- What are some things you have built your life on other than God?
- As a parent, what is one way you can build on God as your Rock?

Living for God's Approval

Am I now trying to win the approval of human beings,
or of God? Or am I trying to please people? If I were still
trying to please people, I would not be a servant of Christ.
—GALATIANS 1:10

Do you ever worry too much about other people's opinions? Maybe you wrestle with what other moms think about your parenting. Or maybe your parent or grandparent seems to judge you. Or maybe that inner voice of your past questions if you'll ever truly measure up as a mom. At times all of us can struggle with living for people's approval instead of living for God's approval.

Even the apostle Paul acknowledged that we can teeter-totter between longing for God's approval and wanting to feel significant in someone else's eyes. It is tempting to let people and their opinions matter more than they really should. We can worry too much about what they think, whether they approve of us, or what we need to do for them to accept us.

This is a dangerous trap though, isn't it?

It is far better to draw our strength from God's approval—to know that in Christ we are fully accepted, fully loved, and fully secure. We have in Him what no one can take away. When honoring Him with our lives matters most to us, other people's acceptance matters less. I love how Thomas à Kempis put it: "Do not be too concerned about who is with you or who is against you, but do be careful that God may be with you in everything you do."[2]

If you are a people-pleaser, remember your top priority is to please God. At the end of our lives, we won't stand before others; we'll stand before God. His assessment, approval, and acceptance will be the only things that matter. Don't let people be bigger than they really are.

Father, help me find my acceptance and approval in You alone. Teach me to value Your opinion of me more than I value the opinion of others. Guard my heart from wanting to please people more than I want to please You. In Jesus' name, amen.

- Why is living for people's approval dangerous to your soul?
- In what aspect of your motherhood are you most tempted right now to live for people's approval more than God's approval?

Carry Each Other's Burdens

Carry each other's burdens, and in this way
you will fulfill the law of Christ.

—GALATIANS 6:2

Several years ago I was rushing through a parking lot carrying several grocery bags when I could feel the bottom of one of the bags beginning to give out. It started as a small tear but was quickly turning into a gaping hole! Any second, my fresh produce would be all over the ground.

My son saw the bag ripping and came running to put his hands underneath the deteriorating paper bag. Just in time, he came alongside me, saving the day (or at least some groceries)!

Parenting often feels like a lot to carry. And it is a lot to hold on to. Motherhood is too hard to do alone, which is why every mom needs close friendships. We all need to be friends and have friends who are willing to "carry each other's burdens."

The word *carry* means to put upon one's self. It is to take what is hard or burdensome for someone else and lift it up for them. A friend who carries something for you is someone who sees you struggling. She knows you are feeling wiped out or overwhelmed. She spots the "bag ripping" and runs to help relieve you, allowing you catch your breath and refuel.

We are called to "carry each other's burdens." We all need friends like that, but we also all need to *be* friends like that. Let's not just be a friend when it's easy. In Christ, we are joined to one another, and sometimes that even means suffering with and for one another.

Father, help me be humble enough to ask for help. Show me where I need someone else's strength, support, or wisdom right now. And help me be the kind of friend who is helping to carry a heavy burden. In Jesus' name, amen.

- Which of your friends is carrying a heavy burden right now? How can you help her?
- Maybe you're carrying a heavy burden. What is one thing you can do today to reach out to a friend and ask for help?

Rest for the Weary

"Come to me, all you who are weary and burdened, and I will
give you rest. Take my yoke upon you and learn from me,
for I am gentle and humble in heart, and you will find rest
for your souls. For my yoke is easy and my burden is light."
—MATTHEW 11:28–30

If there is one thing that all of us moms have in common, it's probably feeling weary and burdened. The degree of weariness may vary from season to season, but still the weariness is there. No wonder Jesus' invitation to come to Him and rest is so appealing.

Jesus said, "Come to me . . . and I will give you rest." Those words got me thinking about how often I do my working, my parenting, my ministry apart from Christ. I try to do too much in my own strength and rely on my own wisdom. Soon I'm carrying things I shouldn't and saying yes to things when I should say no. And yet Jesus invited us to come to Him. Rest is first and foremost about *abiding* in Him.

When we go to Jesus, it's not that we don't work; it's that we work differently. We are to take His yoke upon us and learn from Him. He has promised that when we labor with Him, the weight is different. His yoke is easy, and our burden is much lighter. We experience rest.

Resting in Jesus is trusting Him with what we can't control. Resting in Jesus is living for His approval instead of people's approval. Resting in Jesus is surrendering our plans to His. Resting in Jesus is prayerful dependence. Resting in Jesus is humble obedience.

Are you feeling weary today? Weighed down by burdens? Take Jesus at His word. Take His yoke upon you. He who is humble and gentle has promised that you will find rest for your soul.

Father, You are wiser, more powerful, and more resourceful than I am. Thank You for saving me and sustaining me through Your Son, Jesus. Teach me to abide in You, allowing Your strength to give rest to my soul. Refresh me today. Give me strength to keep going even when life is hard. In Jesus' name, amen.

- What aspect of your life makes you feel most weary today?
- What is one way you can let Jesus carry your burden right now?

A Gift from God

The LORD God caused the man to fall into a deep sleep;
and while he was sleeping, he took one of the man's
ribs and then closed up the place with flesh. Then the
LORD God made a woman from the rib he had taken
out of the man, and he brought her to the man.
—GENESIS 2:21–22

The very first marriage was one that God joined together. The two became one because God first brought the woman to the man (Genesis 2:22). Think about that for a moment. The first marriage was a gift from God. Adam didn't have to go out looking for Eve. He didn't have to court her or pursue her to win her over. Likewise, Eve didn't have to win Adam over or convince him she was the one. God took her to him as a gift. And this gift would change the rest of their lives.

Each of us as couples were joined together or brought together in our own unique ways. But behind the scenes, it was God who was ultimately behind bringing us together. We are God's gift to each other. We have been brought together for the gift of friendship, intimacy, family, and ministry. You and your spouse were not brought together by accident!

While it may not always seem like it, our different strengths, experiences, personalities, and gifts are meant to complement, not compete with, each other. In marriage, we experience the blessing of both receiving one another and giving to one another. Ask God to help you see your spouse as a gift. Ask Him to help you love one another and serve one another. In marriage, we are God's gift to each other!

Father, You have given my husband to me as a gift. Help me not to compete with him but to complement him. I pray that You would strengthen our marriage today by helping the two of us see each other as a gift from You and treat each other that way. In Jesus' name, amen.

- List some specific reasons why you consider your spouse a gift.
- What is one way you can shore up your husband's weaknesses with your strengths?

take Fun More Seriously

She is clothed with strength and dignity;
she can laugh at the days to come.
—PROVERBS 31:25

Is your home a fun place to live? How would your kids answer that question? Their answers may tell us moms that it's time we take fun a little more seriously!

I know, I know, motherhood is stressful and exhausting. Still, let's not fail to give our kids the gifts of laughter, fun, and lightheartedness. We can be at ease because we know our wise and loving God is in control. Who He is changes who we are.

It might surprise you, but the Bible describes the Proverbs 31 woman, who is a person of character, as a woman who knows how to laugh. Among all of her responsibilities and activities, we're told she was able to "laugh at the days to come." She was not ruled by fear, consumed with worry, overcome with weariness, or worn out by preparing for what was ahead. She laughed not because she was a good comedian, but because she trusted the God who is in control.

What a great reminder for you and me! In this demanding mission of motherhood, we can sometimes take life too seriously. We can take our calling as moms too seriously. As a result, we can fail to enjoy this journey. Our fear of tomorrow can rob us of joy and laughter today. As serious as being a mom can be, let's be sure to have some fun along the way!

Our homes are to be a safe haven and a place of refuge for our kids. But let's also be more intentional about making our homes fun places to be. Filling our homes with joy. Playing with our kids. Laughing with our kids because we know who is really ruling the world.

Father, please help me remember throughout the day that You are in control. Don't let fear or worry rob me of my joy. Fill our home with laughter. Let it be a place of joy and peace because of whom we know You to be. In Jesus' name, amen.

- Do you think your kids would describe your home as fun? Why or why not?
- What are one or two things you can do to bring more fun or laughter into your home?

Simple Obedience

These were all commended for their faith, yet none
of them received what had been promised, since
God had planned something better for us so that only
together with us would they be made perfect.
—HEBREWS 11:39–40

Don't go out and try to do something great.

It might sound strange. Maybe even a little backward. But stick with me here!

I love the Hebrews 11 list of men and women who lived by faith. Each person, while acting in faith, wasn't necessarily trying to do something big or great. When God spoke, they simply obeyed.

By faith, Noah built a boat. By faith, Abraham left his home. By faith, Moses' parents hid him for three months. By faith, the Israelites passed through the Red Sea. By faith, Rahab welcomed and hid a few spies on the run.

All significant acts of faith. Steps of obedience. Some of the actions were risky. Others seemed crazy to a watching world. But what is worth noting about these people is that they weren't trying to do great things.

They were simply trying to be obedient. They heard God's call, and they responded with obedience.

Where is God calling you to do the same? Is your focus on trying to do something big or great? Or are you focusing on being obedient? No matter where God has you or what He calls you to do, do it. Success in God's eyes is obedience. So be faithful today. Listen for God's voice. Step out in faith. Don't worry about doing great things. Be faithful, obey, and let God do the rest!

Father, help me focus more on obeying You than doing something great. Thank You for the reminder that obedience, no matter how small the act, is success in Your eyes. By faith, I want to honor You, be used by You, and show a watching world what You are really like. In Jesus' name, amen.

- Why is it wrong to focus on doing something great?
- In what ways does God reward you for your faith (Hebrews 11:6)?

God Uses Your Weakness

Three times I pleaded with the Lord to take it away
from me. But he said, "My grace is sufficient for you,
for my power is made perfect in weakness."
—2 CORINTHIANS 12:8–9

There are plenty of opportunities for a mom to feel weak. When we haven't managed to hop into the shower—and it's time to make dinner. When we arrive late for Bible study . . . with no shoes for the toddler. When we see on Facebook another mom's cupcakes for her child's birthday party. When we end the day by counting how many balls we dropped.

For the longest time, I resisted my weakness. After all, who is proud of not having everything figured out? But God actually has a purpose for our weakness. It's like a door that allows God to enter and begin a work in us we would never have experienced if we faked being strong. As it turns out, admitting our weakness is the first step to relying on God and not ourselves.

In the New Testament we see that the apostle Paul, in a season of intense hardship and weakness, pleaded with God to take "it" away.

Nobody is entirely certain what Paul's "it" was, but whatever it was, Paul was feeling weak.

We all have an "it." More often than not, God transforms us in our weakness instead of taking our weakness away. He transforms us by using our weakness to teach us to rely on Him and not on our own strength or wisdom. He doesn't wait for us to become strong, secure, confident, or healthy. God does His greatest work in and through our weakness.

God responded to Paul's pleading with the promise that His grace and His life-giving power were enough. So, if you feel weak today, you are exactly where God wants you! Whatever you are facing, remember that God loves to reveal His power through weakness. His power is made perfect in those of us who don't feel as if we can do it all on our own.

Father, instead of taking away my weakness, transform me. Use my weakness to teach me to rely on You, resting in Your strength and wisdom. Your grace is enough for me today. In Jesus' name, amen.

- In what ways might God use your weakness to bring about growth as a mom?
- How is embracing your weakness not the same as being indifferent?

Establishing Traditions

"These are the LORD's appointed festivals, the sacred
assemblies you are to proclaim at their appointed times."
—LEVITICUS 23:4

One of my favorite family traditions growing up was going to my grandparents' house on Sunday nights. They lived about twenty minutes away from us, and each Sunday, we'd load up our car and head to their house for dinner. We'd share a meal and then sit in their living room and talk. It wasn't anything fancy, but this weekly rhythm had a lasting impact on me.

Traditions can be powerful and practical ways for families to pass on values, celebrate important events, or create memories. Most often, traditions are associated with different holidays. We can be intentional as a family, just as God's people were in the past, about establishing traditions that have spiritual meaning.

In the Old Testament book of Leviticus, God commanded His people to observe a series of seven feasts. These became annual traditions, filled with feasting, celebrating, offering sacrifices, and at times, confessing sins. Each of these traditions was primarily meant to pass along, from generation to generation, truths about who God is and what God had done. These were yearly opportunities for God's people to refocus on His love, truth, and faithfulness. These feasts also pointed to what Jesus would one day do for all people.

Traditions, simple or elaborate, can leave a lasting imprint. Simple traditions may not always seem like much to us, but they can be a lasting legacy for our children. What are some simple and practical traditions that you can create for your family? More importantly, how can these yearly practices be used to pass on faith? How can your family traditions continue to point your kids toward who Jesus is and all that He has done?

Father, I confess that it is easy to forget all You have done. Help me remember Your goodness and faithfulness. As I create traditions in my family, use them to help pass on faith to my kids and grandkids. In Jesus' name, amen.

- What family tradition had the most impact on you when you were growing up? Why was it so significant?
- What is one way you can begin establishing family traditions in your home?

the Holiness of God

Just as he who called you is holy, so be holy in all you do.
—1 PETER 1:15

There is no one like God. He is far above all creation. He is completely unique in His character. Unmatched in His worth. He has many opponents, but no one is His rival. He is, and always will be, "holy, holy, holy" (Isaiah 6:3).

The holiness of God reminds us that He is different from us. He reigns and rules from heaven, while we live here on earth. He is perfect in all His ways. He always does what is good, pleasing, and right. Unlike us, He is pure, faithful, righteous, and without sin. And yet, by faith in Christ, God shares His holiness with us.

In and through Jesus, the Holy One makes us holy. Jesus' purity covers our impurity. Jesus' faithfulness covers our unfaithfulness. Our lack of holiness is swallowed up at the cross. Instead of our unrighteousness, Jesus clothes us with His. In Christ, God declares us set apart.

Peter reminded us that "he who called you is holy." But Peter didn't stop there. He knew that Jesus had made His people holy, and through

His Spirit, He is still making us holy. So Peter continued, "Be holy in all you do."

The holiness of God should cause us to worship. To walk humbly. To rejoice in our forgiveness. But it should also motivate us to give back what God has so graciously given us in Christ. He has made us holy, so let's be holy, set apart, fully devoted to God in all we do!

Father, there is no one like You. You alone are worthy of my praise. You are the Creator and King over all creation. You are perfect in all Your ways. Thank You for forgiving my sin, making me clean, setting me apart in Christ by faith, and making me holy. I want to honor, revere, and serve You in all I do. In Jesus' name, amen.

- Have you become too casual with God in any ways?
- In what ways can the holiness of God motivate your parenting?

When You Don't Feel Like Being a Mom

"Whoever loses their life for my sake will find it."
—MATTHEW 10:39

What do you do when you don't feel like being a mom? How do you handle those days, weeks, or maybe months when you secretly wish you were doing anything else but changing diapers, chauffeuring kids, and listening to sibling squabbles?

I thought motherhood would always come easily. I imagined that the mothering instinct to love, care for, and nurture would be continually present and consistent. It would always feel natural. But I was wrong. The truth is, from time to time, a lot of moms don't want to be moms.

In Matthew, Jesus gave us a helpful, if not hard, reminder. The problem is not in our parenting; the problem is in our hearts. Being a mom isn't what satisfies our hearts; it's knowing and serving Christ. What quenches the thirst we all feel is walking in obedience wherever God has us.

As God is patiently growing us and transforming us, He is changing us from the inside out. He gently redirects us from what we think we want to what He knows we actually need. Our hearts will always be restless and wandering until we learn that only hungering and thirsting for God will truly satisfy.

When we don't feel like being moms, we need to remember the problem is not motherhood; the problem is how we view what will truly satisfy. The blessed life, the abundant life (John 10:10), is not found in doing what we want. It's found, Jesus said, in giving our lives away. It's found in sacrificially loving and serving. We find life when we lose our lives. The good life is found in loving God and others, even when we don't always feel like it! The promise, though, is good. He has promised to satisfy us with good things, even better things than what we thought.

Father, fill me with good things. Forgive me for often pursuing what I want, rather than what You want for me. Teach me to desire You. I know that only You can truly satisfy my soul. Come and fill me today with Your love, joy, and peace. In Jesus' name, amen.

- How have you ever struggled with not wanting to be a mom?
- What is one thing you can do today to hunger and thirst for God?

A Sneaky Form of Pride

Do not think of yourself more highly than you ought, but
rather think of yourself with sober judgment, in accordance
with the faith God has distributed to each of you.
—ROMANS 12:3

What's the big deal with pride? It has been said that pride is really at the root of all other sins. The most hidden and secret of all sins, pride is easy to see in others but hard to spot in ourselves. The real problem with pride, though, is that it is an attempt to elevate ourselves above God.

I'm guessing we've all been around prideful people. They exalt themselves, talk about themselves, and promote themselves every chance they get. That kind of pride is what we might call self-promotion. We've all been guilty of those things at times.

But that's not the only form pride takes. A sneakier kind of pride takes the form of self-loathing.

We see self-loathing in the person who is always putting herself down. She thinks she's no good at being a mom. Her kids will never turn out okay. Her pants are too tight. The birthday party was a failure. Her house is smaller and dirtier than everyone else's on the block. In other words, she is always down on herself. Every day is the perfect day for a pity party. This self-loathing is a form of pride because it is a fixation on self. Whenever we put ourselves down or talk about how bad we have it, we are really sneakily drawing the focus and attention back to us.

To one degree or another, we all wrestle with pride. Both forms of pride—self-promotion and self-loathing—interfere with loving God and loving others. In either case, we're too busy thinking about ourselves.

Which form of pride do you wrestle with? Ask God today to help you become less fixated on yourself and more focused on loving Him and loving others. He's promised to give you grace where you need it most.

Lord, You alone are worthy of praise and honor. Please help me take my eyes off of myself. Give me grace to walk in humility, focusing more on loving You and loving others. In Jesus' name, amen.

- In what ways have you seen pride—self-promotion or self-loathing—take root in your heart as a mom?
- What can you do today to be more focused on God and less preoccupied with yourself?

A Friend Worth Following

Remember your leaders, who spoke the word
of God to you. Consider the outcome of
their way of life and imitate their faith.

—HEBREWS 13:7

The church is a community of people in which God's Spirit dwells. God works through His people to teach us and guide us. We don't need just anybody to surround us. We need godly people who walk by the Spirit and know the truth of God's Word, people who are humble and honest. These kinds of friends are a rare gift.

Although Hebrews 13:7 is talking about remembering our leaders, we could apply this verse to remembering godly and wise friends as well. The writer told us to remember and think about the people whose lives are actually worth following. "Consider the outcome of their way of life," the writer said. Evaluate their marriages. Think about their character. Watch them live out their faith. Look at their families. Listen to their speech. Notice the fruit of their faithfulness to God. And if all that's in line with God's Word, learn from their example. Follow them as they follow Jesus.

We all need a friend or two who is further down the road, wiser, godly, and willing to pour into us. Very rarely will these kinds of friends approach us. If we want to surround ourselves with these kinds of friends, we will need to be intentional and seek them out. Maybe it looks like a cup of coffee once a month, an occasional lunch, or just a phone call for advice. Don't wait for this type of friend. Seek her out!

Who are you following? Who is it in your life, your church, or community that you would want to imitate? We become better through the people we choose to surround ourselves with.

Father, give me wisdom to seek out the friends who will help me become more like Jesus. Show me the women I might reach out to for wisdom, encouragement, or advice. Lord, bless me with the kind of friends who will make me better, more like Jesus. You know what I need, so lead me to a faithful friend who is worth following. In Jesus' name, amen.

- Who do you know who is a friend worth following?
- What younger mom or woman could you reach out to for coffee or lunch? Who might God be calling you to pour into?

Pursuing Godliness

Have nothing to do with godless myths and old wives'
tales; rather, train yourself to be godly. For physical training
is of some value, but godliness has value for all things.
—1 TIMOTHY 4:7–8

Several years ago I decided to train for and run a 5K. I am not a runner at all, so this was not something that came naturally to me. To train for the big event, I disciplined myself to work hard each day. I became committed to stretching, running, and eating right. I also disciplined myself not to do certain things, like sleeping in later and eating certain foods. Although I never did run an actual race, I did well with the training, and I was thankful I stuck with it.

It's not surprising that the Bible uses the language of training and discipline for describing the Christian life. After all, nobody accidentally becomes like Jesus. It takes work and discipline. If we want to experience all that God has for us, we need to train ourselves to be godly.

Training doesn't mean we work in order to get God's approval. We already have His acceptance by faith in what Jesus has done for us (Ephesians 2:8–9). Training is living a life committed to Jesus and focused on Him. Training involves working out our salvation, pursuing the goal of godliness out of gratitude for all God has done for us.

Now look at what the rest of 1 Timothy 4:8 says: "Godliness has value for all things, holding promise for both the present life and the life to come." Not only does godliness benefit us in the life to come, but it benefits us now. The pursuit of godliness is of great value to our own soul as well as to the people around us. Our families are blessed by the fruit of our desire to be like Christ.

Start training today. Devote yourself to godliness. You will be blessed by it, and so will your family.

Father, the life You offer me is abundant. I know that You have saved me by grace because of my faith in Jesus. Help me pursue You with all I have. Show me what is hindering me, and teach me to train myself to pursue godliness. In Jesus' name, amen.

- What are some specific ways you can "train yourself to be godly"?
- What do you need to put off or get rid of in order to pursue godliness?

trusting God together

Trust in the LORD with all your heart and lean not on
your own understanding; in all your ways submit
to him, and he will make your paths straight.

—PROVERBS 3:5–6

Soon after I got married I learned that my desire to be in control was going to make life a lot more difficult. I suddenly had my husband's wants and needs to take into consideration. Over time I learned that my need to control wasn't so much about me or my spouse but ultimately about my trust in God, or lack thereof.

When we try to control our situation rather than trusting God, we can create a lot of unnecessary stress and tension in our marriages. A couple facing difficult times might be tempted to fight against, instead of fighting for, each other.

We are invited to trust the Lord with all of our hearts. We are told to "lean not" on our own knowledge or resources, but to put all our confidence in God coming through for us. Hold on to Him. The promise is that He will make our paths straight.

Where do you and your spouse need to trust God? What challenges are you facing that you need to let God carry? Is there stress or tension, maybe even conflict, because one or both of you are not trusting God?

Today, pray that your marriage would be marked with trust—a confidence in God's plans and timing. Pray against letting stress, fear, or worry burden your marriage. Ask the Father to carry what is heavy. Lean on Him and ask Him to continue to direct your steps as you trust Him at every twist and turn.

Father, we don't always understand what You are doing or why You are doing it, but don't let the difficult and hard things tear us apart. You know what is best for us. You are stronger, wiser, more resourceful, and good. Help us love each other more as we learn to lean on You. In Jesus' name, amen.

- In what ways are you struggling to trust God in your marriage right now?
- What is one step you and your spouse can take to trust God and to "lean not on your own understanding"?

Do Something Brave

Have I not commanded you? Be strong and courageous.
Do not be afraid; do not be discouraged, for the Lord
your God will be with you wherever you go.
—JOSHUA 1:9

What do you dream about doing but are too afraid to try? Is there something you've always wanted to do, but you feel inadequate or unqualified? If so, maybe today is the day you need to go for it and do something brave!

But don't just do something brave for your own sake; do it for God. Living the Christian life in a way that impacts people around us can be uncomfortable, even risky. Whether in our workplaces, neighborhoods, or churches, we may have to step out of what is predictable or familiar and trust God for the outcome.

In what way is God calling you to be brave? Maybe it's inviting a neighbor over for dinner. It could be reaching out to a coworker. Or perhaps it is speaking up in conversations around the office or at the playground when you've been silent. It might be leading a Bible study, serving in a different kind of ministry, or getting together with another mom in your neighborhood.

Fear paralyzes us and keeps us stuck. It robs us of the joy of walking in faith. Being brave doesn't mean we don't have any fears or insecurities. Being brave means doing something regardless of our fears.

We can find the strength to do something brave for God's sake when we remember the promise that He is with us wherever we go. We never step out by ourselves or in our own power.

So whatever God is calling you to do, remember He is not calling you to do it alone. "Be strong and courageous . . . for the LORD your God will be with you wherever you go."

Lord, give me courage to step out in faith today. I don't want to live a comfortable or predictable Christian life. I want to be brave, but brave because of my trust in You. Help me remember that wherever You lead me, You also empower me to do the task You have for me. In Jesus' name, amen.

- What is God calling you to do that you have been too fearful to do before?
- What is one thing you can do today to step out in faith for God's glory?

Understanding Anger

In your anger do not sin.
—EPHESIANS 4:26

*E*very mom starts out oohing and aahing over her child. And then reality kicks in. The demands and challenges of raising another human being bring out stuff in us that we didn't even know was there! This is all a part of God's plan to change us from the inside out.

As every mom knows, anger is one of those dangerous emotions lurking in our hearts. Not all anger is sinful in God's eyes. After all, God gets angry too. But His anger is always good and right. Unlike ours, His anger is over what is right and pure.

Our sinful anger, on the other hand, is self-centered. Rather than revolving around what is right, our anger is based on what we want. Anger is a nasty emotion that can either explode in an instant or simmer beneath the surface until is slowly oozes out of every pore of our being. But what often drives our sinful anger is wanting something more than we want God.

Sinful anger is always connected to something we hold important. We want comfort and don't get it, so we get angry. We want control and don't have it, so we get angry. We want respect or approval, and when we don't get it, we get angry. While those things aren't inherently bad, they can become idols to us. Our sinful anger is the result of our wanting something more than we want God Himself.

So when you start to feel that hot flash of anger, stop and ask yourself, *What is it that I really want right now? What am I desiring more than loving God and loving others? Is this righteous anger or sinful anger?* Remember Paul's words: "In your anger do not sin." And rest in the promise that you have all you need in God.

Father, forgive me for the times I get angry for the wrong reasons. Search my heart and show me those desires that are sinful and self-centered. Teach me to be slow to anger, kind, patient, and compassionate. Change me from the inside out. In Jesus' name, amen.

- Why is God's righteous anger an expression of His love?
- What does your anger reveal about what you truly desire?

Nourishing Your Children's Souls

Jesus answered, "It is written: 'Man shall
not live on bread alone, but on every word
that comes from the mouth of God.'"

—MATTHEW 4:4

As the years march by, our kids are not the only ones growing—so is our food budget. All four of our kids love to eat. Keeping a pantry well-stocked is nearly impossible, especially with two teenagers! The Bible has a lot to say about eating—not just eating to satisfy physical hunger, but our spiritual hunger as well.

We are hungry and thirsty. And yet the Bible reminds us that all of this language of eating and drinking is really about our deeper need. Our deepest longings. Our souls' thirst and hunger for God. We will never be truly satisfied until we come to know and treasure Jesus, the true Bread of life (John 6:35).

Our kids do not come into the world knowing what to do with their hunger and thirst. They need us to lead them, teach them, protect them, and help them know Jesus. Just like us, they will try to fill their hunger with relationships, stuff, entertainment, accomplishments, and countless distractions. Patiently and persistently, we must keep bringing them back to God's Word and His unconditional love, abounding grace, and faithful promises.

We are not just raising kids; we are shaping their souls. And just as we would never send them into the world without physical nourishment, we can't send them into the world starved of spiritual nourishment either. Let's remember to feed our kids. Read God's Word with them. Help them memorize His truth. Remind them of His love. Bury His promises in their hearts. Feed their stomachs, but most importantly, nourish their souls.

Father, I believe Your Word satisfies those who hunger and thirst for righteousness. Continue to create in me a hunger to know You and love You. Give me wisdom and strength to nourish my kids' souls. Help me not to grow weary, become complacent, or stop being alert. Remind me to diligently feed and nourish my children's hearts with Your truth. In Jesus' name, amen.

- How can you protect your kids with God's Word?
- What is one way you can begin nourishing your child's soul today with God's Word?

Our Helper

The Lord is my helper; I will not be afraid.
What can mere mortals do to me?
—HEBREWS 13:6

One way God loves us is by listening to us. He knows when we are afraid. He turns His ear to us when we are overwhelmed. When we feel like we're in over our heads, He is not indifferent. He not only hears us, but He also helps us.

To say that God is our Helper is to admit we are lacking wisdom and strength. To cry out to God as our Helper is to go to the One who has infinite resources to supply what we need. The writer of Hebrews reminds us that we can have total confidence that, regardless of the circumstances, God will never leave us or forsake us. We can declare, "The Lord is my helper; I will not be afraid."

God is our defender. Protector. Provider. The source of our strength.

We say it with confidence and conviction: we will not be afraid. As Paul asked, "If God is for us, who can be against us?" (Romans 8:31). When we need help, we have Someone who comes to our aid. He is with us, and He is for us. He is our Helper.

What are you struggling with right now? Where do you feel weak? Is something in your work, your parenting, your marriage, or your family making you feel helpless? One of the most important and powerful prayers we can pray is simply, "Lord, help me."

Ask God to take away any traces of unbelief, to be with you in your marriage and in your mothering. He will enable you to be steadfast, diligent, and faithful. Turn to Him to guard your heart; He is your ever-present Helper. You can have full confidence in the fact that He is who He says He is, and He will do all that He says He will do.

Lord, You are my Helper. You have promised that You will never leave me or forsake me. Help me in my weakness. Supply what is lacking in me. Pour out Your power and wisdom in me so that I can be the mom You have called me to be. Lord, I love You and trust You. In Jesus' name, amen.

- What is causing you to feel helpless right now?
- What is one thing you can do today to rely on God's help?

From Greed To Giving

[Jesus] said to them, "Watch out! Be on your
guard against all kinds of greed; life does not
consist in an abundance of possessions."
—LUKE 12:15

W atch out!" I yelled from our front porch. Unfortunately, my warning came a little too late. Sophia, our youngest child, was cruising down the side of the street on her scooter when I noticed the large pothole directly in her path. Just as I was warning her, she was hitting it!

As it turns out, moms are not the only protective ones. Even Jesus told His followers to watch out on occasion.

In one of those times, He warned us about greed. The desire for too much stuff is not always as easy to identify in ourselves as it is in other people. So we have to be on guard and watch out for the different ways we can desire to own too much stuff or allow our stuff to own us.

Jesus said we are to be on guard against "all kinds of greed." This phrase implies that we can be stingy with more than just our treasure. We can hold too tightly to our possessions and our money. But we can also become tightfisted with our time, never giving away minutes or hours to others. We can also hold on to our gifts, not allowing God to use the talents and passions He has given us to bless others.

Each day we have countless opportunities to live greedily or generously. We serve a God who became poor to make us rich (2 Corinthians 8:9). He has given us far more than we deserve! Vow to live more generously today and to live with less so you can give more.

Father, You have blessed me more than I deserve. You have been generous to me. In Christ, You have saved me, forgiven me, and given me peace and hope. Help me give to others because You have given so much to me. In Jesus' name, amen.

- Where do you struggle the most with greed? Is it with your time, gifts, or money?
- What are some ways you can live more generously today?

Friends Who Tell the Truth

Love does not delight in evil but rejoices with the truth.

—1 CORINTHIANS 13:6

"I'm not sure I wanted to hear that," I told my friend, "but I needed to hear it." An older mom and dear friend had just given me a rare gift: the truth. I was struggling. Feeling exhausted. Honestly, I was hoping to have my thoughts and feelings validated. But instead of encouraging me and empathizing with me (which she did), she did something more, something far more valuable.

With compassion, my friend sliced through what I was feeling and thinking to speak truth to me. She gave me the reality check I desperately needed!

We all need friends like this friend of mine. Friends who will love us. Pray for us. Encourage us. Listen closely to us and help us carry our burdens when we feel overwhelmed. But one of the most loving things a friend can do is help us temper our thoughts, feelings, and actions with God's truth.

Love desires to see a friend grow. It listens, feels, clarifies, uplifts, but always desires change. A friend who loves us and tells us the truth is willing to risk hurting our feelings for the sake of seeing us grow. Jesus taught that the truth sets us free (John 8:32). It sets us free from dangerous habits, toxic emotions, and unhealthy thoughts, enabling us to become better moms in the process.

Do we really want friends who only tell us what we want to hear? Is it really good for our own hearts, marriages, or families? The foundation of any good and God-honoring friendship is truth. Let's build our friendships wisely by building them with love and truth.

Father, thank You for knowing the truth about me and loving me anyway. Show me where I am not walking in the truth. Are there actions, thoughts, or feelings that are not correct? Give me friends who will help me see, think, and feel clearly, enabling me to experience the freedom Your truth brings. In Jesus' name, amen.

- Why is it not truly loving to say only what friends want to hear?
- What is one way you can begin building more truth, along with love, into your friendships?

More than a Song

I urge you, brothers and sisters, in view of God's mercy,
to offer your bodies as a living sacrifice, holy and
pleasing to God—this is your true and proper worship.
—ROMANS 12:1

I grew up singing, and still to this day worshipping God through song is one of my favorite things to do. But the New Testament instructs us that worship is bigger, more consuming than just singing songs. Worship is to be a way of life, a posture of the heart, set on loving God and loving others. This is "true and proper worship."

Romans 12:1 is a reminder that a life of worship is a response. Paul wrote, "In view of God's mercy, to offer your bodies as a living sacrifice." It is a reaction to and for God. The only appropriate reaction to all that God has done for us in Christ is to give our lives back to Him. To worship Him.

We are to offer ourselves—our attitudes, speech, desires of our hearts, and the members of our bodies—in such a way that they are holy and pleasing to God. Every routine, seen and unseen, is to be an act of worship to the God who is worthy of it all.

In motherhood, countless moments seem ordinary. Folding clothes. Helping with homework. Doing the dishes. Teaching and instructing. Yet when done with a heart positioned to love God and love others, everyday moments are sacred. Just imagine how different today could be if we saw each moment as a moment meant for worship.

Worship God with your songs today. But don't stop there. Worship Him in all you do, as a living sacrifice that is holy and pleasing to the Lord.

Father, in light of Your great mercy, help me offer my body to You as a living sacrifice. Take my thoughts, my words, my hands, and my feet. I am offering all of who I am to You today. I want my life to be an offering to You, one that is holy and pleasing. In Jesus' name, amen.

- In what area of your life do you most need the reminder that all of life is meant to be worship?
- What can you do to make the ordinary routines of motherhood moments of worship?

Yielding in Love

Submit to one another out of reverence for Christ.
—EPHESIANS 5:21

*I*n the past, whenever I thought of the word *submit*, I had visions of an army waving a white flag in defeat. *Submission* was never a positive word to me. It was a sign of defeat. But nothing could be further from the truth. To submit simply means to yield.

Recently, we were driving to the store and someone coming into our lane decided to ignore the yield sign. The result was almost disastrous! Yield signs are necessary for preventing countless accidents and collisions.

In marriage, submitting is about learning to yield in love to your spouse. Failing to yield in love to each other can be as dangerous as two cars fighting over the right of way. In fact, many marital conflicts are birthed out of a desire to be right or get our way. Submission, however, requires learning to be a servant-lover of our spouses.

Jesus is the ultimate example of One who submitted His life to the Father. In love, Jesus yielded His desires and will to the Father's in order to bring us life through His death and resurrection. In marriage, we are to follow in Jesus' footsteps, yielding to each other out of love.

Today, follow Jesus' footsteps. Be willing to serve. Resist the temptation to always have to be right or in control. Ask God to give you the power to live like Jesus in your marriage. Ask that He might give you a servant's heart—a heart that is growing in love.

Father, teach me to be like Your Son. Help me yield to my spouse in our marriage. Help us not to expect perfection from each other, but humbly serve one another. Give me the grace to resist wanting my way all the time. Empower me to lay down my life out of love for my spouse. In Jesus' name, amen.

- What is the biggest reason you struggle to yield in love to your spouse?
- What is one simple way you can begin yielding in love to your spouse?

Greater than Darkness

You, Lord, keep my lamp burning; my
God turns my darkness into light.
—PSALM 18:28

*O*n my way to the kitchen early one morning, I passed the room of my oldest daughter, Bella. Stopping to pull the door shut so I wouldn't wake her, I noticed a small glow of light.

As I peeked in, I noticed the book light clipped to her headboard from her late-night reading. The lamp had shifted in the night and now was shining, like a spotlight, on Bella, who was sound asleep. The light was just enough to carve out some of the darkness.

When we open the Bible, we discover that God has been pushing back darkness from the very beginning. When He said, "Let there be light" in Genesis 1:3, it is better to read it as, "There will be light." It was literally a command for the darkness to flee.

No matter how old we are, darkness can be scary. The "lights" go out, and we find ourselves in a season of despair. We're disoriented. Unsure about what to do. Afraid of what may be ahead. But in the darkness, God does not leave us. He is still pushing it back and filling it with light—filling the darkness with Himself.

When darkness threatens to overtake us and we can't see, it's important for us to remember who we are following. God gives us His Word. His promises. His heart. And ultimately He gave us His Son. Jesus called Himself the "light of the world" (John 8:12). He was, He is, and He always will be! If we are in Him, we are never truly walking in darkness.

God doesn't give us a map, but He gave us His Son. We must turn to Jesus, the only One who can turn our darkness into light.

Father, You have promised never to leave me or forsake me. Your Word is like a lamp for my feet. Your Son is the Light of the world. Even when I can't see You or understand what You are doing, help me hold on to these truths and keep trusting You. In Jesus' name, amen.

- In what ways can God use seasons of darkness to transform you?
- In what ways do you resist God when life doesn't make sense or the path doesn't seem clear?

Learning to Truly Love

This is how we know what love is: Jesus Christ
laid down his life for us. And we ought to lay
down our lives for our brothers and sisters.
—1 JOHN 3:16

Have you ever felt unappreciated as a mom? Have you ever felt frustrated by your kids' seeming indifference about all you do for them? Guess what? You are not alone. And it's tough to love when you don't always get a return.

Of course, at times we get a cute card, a text message, or a thank-you. But more often than not, what we do seems to go unnoticed and unappreciated. So we need to guard our hearts against our quiet pity parties. We need to see that God is using motherhood to do something glorious in us: He is making us more like Christ. The heart work that God wants to do in us is to teach us how to love as He loves.

As we pour ourselves out for our children, God is changing us and giving us a deeper understanding of true love. With the help of His Spirit, God enables us to love for the sake of someone else. He is turning us outward when we could easily turn inward.

Yes, true love is costly and sacrificial. It requires that we lay down our lives for our children, and this kind of love gives—even if no one notices. After all, God first loved us, long before we ever loved Him back. May we as moms learn to love like that.

Father, I confess that I am still learning how to truly love. Forgive me for the times when I love with the expectation of getting something in return. I can't love the way I want to love on my own, so give me Your strength to love sacrificially. Give me grace to love for the good of others and not just for what I might get in return. Help me lay down my life just as Jesus laid down His life for me. In Jesus' name, amen.

- Appreciation and respect are good things, but how can they become idols?
- Take a minute and read 1 John 3:16 again. In what ways are moms to imitate Christ's love?

God Loves the Real You

See what great love the Father has lavished on us, that we
should be called children of God! And that is what we are!
—1 JOHN 3:1

A parent's voice is powerful, isn't it? I love that we belong to a Father who is not silent. He is a Father who not only speaks *to* His children, but speaks *over* His children. In 1 John 3:1, I find it interesting that the apostle John added the phrase, "And that is what we are!" We might not always believe, feel, or truly comprehend that God loves us enough to call us His children, but our Father says we really are!

Our Father doesn't just love us; He loves the real us. We can act as if we have it all together when sometimes we don't. We can pretend we aren't struggling when we really are. If we're honest, we can hide those areas of our lives where we are still growing. But we don't need to do that with God. Because we are in Christ, forgiven and righteous through His sacrifice, we are loved. Completely. Our Father knows us—all of us—and still loves us.

To make sure we remember our Father's love when it gets hard to hear His voice, He put His Spirit inside us (Romans 8:14–17). The Spirit helps us hear the truth about who and what we really are. His voice reminds us that we are not only forgiven, but we are accepted. We are adopted into God's family. We are His daughters.

If you are in Christ, look and see what great love the Father has lavished on you. This love calls you "My daughter." You are family. May His love for you ring loudly in your ears today: you are His. He loves you—the real you.

Father, thank You for loving me. You know everything about me. You see the areas where I'm still growing, and You are patient, kind, and compassionate to me. Help me not to run from You, but to run to You. Your grace and love are what I need. In Jesus' name, amen.

- In what ways do you hide or pretend you are doing okay when you really aren't?
- Why is it so freeing to know that God loves you, the *real* you?

Weak Spots

Do not give the devil a foothold.
—EPHESIANS 4:27

Our family set out with great enthusiasm. We lathered up in sunscreen. Put on our sunglasses. Made sure our life jackets were securely fastened. And off we went down the river in our kayaks.

I realized later, however, that there was a problem: I failed to put sunscreen on the tops of my knees. Four hours later, I could barely touch them. They were torched. To this day, when we are on the water, I put sunscreen on my knees first.

I learned a lesson that day: we can be almost completely protected, but all it takes for damage to be done is exposure in a single spot. That's all our enemy needs.

Part of what makes the spiritual life challenging is that we have a very real spiritual enemy. He is not indifferent to us, nor is he apathetic toward our calling as moms. First Peter 5:8 says Satan "prowls around . . . looking for someone to devour." All he needs is one spot to get a foothold.

The enemy doesn't need all of your emotions. Just one. He doesn't need all of your relationships. Just one. He doesn't need all of your pleasures. Just one. He doesn't need all of us. Our enemy needs only one weak spot. With only one area unprotected and exposed, Satan can get a foothold in our lives.

We don't need to be scared, but we do want to be wise. In your parenting, be alert and stand firm in your faith.

Father, give me Your grace to stand firm. Fill me with Your Spirit, who I know is greater and more powerful than the enemy. Give me wisdom to know where I am vulnerable. I ask for Your power and protection over my marriage, family, and home. In Jesus' name, amen.

- What does it mean for the devil to get a "foothold" in your life?
- What do you need to do today in order to walk wisely and be protected from the enemy?

Friendships Need Forgiveness

Bear with each other and forgive one another
if any of you has a grievance against someone.
Forgive as the Lord forgave you.
—COLOSSIANS 3:13

Friendships without forgiveness will never last. Conflict inevitably arises in even the best relationships. We say things we regret. We act out of pride, insecurity, or the desire to be in control. These are just a few of the reasons why forgiveness is so important in every friendship.

We are commanded to "bear with each other." To bear with one another means to endure. We are to be the kind of friend who sticks with the relationship. We don't give up early or easily when a friendship gets messy. And key to bearing with each other is the willingness to forgive.

Understand that forgiveness doesn't mean sweeping hurt under the rug. We don't minimize an offense. If we have been wronged, we acknowledge the pain and go to the person, seeking to reconcile and make right the wrong that was done. At that point, forgiveness is a decision to let the offense go. We make a conscious choice not to make that person pay for what she has done to us.

Choosing to forgive doesn't mean we no longer remember or feel the hurt. But when we ask God, He will provide the strength we need to allow our love to cover over a sin, misunderstanding, or conflict. Forgiveness enables us to maintain a relationship we value or treasure.

Is there someone you need to forgive? Do you struggle to stick with a friendship when it gets hard? I encourage you to be a friend who endures. Bear with your friends out of your love for one another. Be quick to acknowledge your own sin and quick to forgive when you are sinned against.

Father, thank You for Your grace. Thank You for the gift of friendship. I pray that You would help me be patient, compassionate, and always willing to forgive when my friendships get messy. Fill me with Your Spirit so that I might be able to show the same kind of love and forgiveness You have shown me. In Jesus' name, amen.

- Why do we often find it difficult to have long-lasting friendships?
- If there is someone you need to forgive, what is one step you can take today to extend forgiveness?

Hope that Will Not Disappoint

"I am the Lord; those who hope in me
will not be disappointed."
—ISAIAH 49:23

Have you ever noticed that it is much easier to live at the beginning of something than it is to live in the middle? Whether it is in a sport, relationship, activity, or even motherhood, we often start out with great enthusiasm. But then the race gets longer. The friendship gets rockier. Or we discover being a mom isn't all grins and giggles. We hit the middle. We discover that living faithfully in the middle can be really difficult.

It is often in the middle when we need the most hope. Hope that we are not alone. Hope that things are not really out of control. Hope that God is still good, powerful, and at work, even if we can't always see it. We need the assurance that God is for us and with us. We need to remember that the middle has an ending, and God will once again dwell with us, heal us, and fully restore us.

In his letter to the Romans, the apostle Paul explained that our hope is not merely wishful thinking (8:32). The assurance of our hope is found in the fact that God gave His Son. Our hope is secure because Jesus was crucified and resurrected for us. This hope is enough to keep us going, even in the middle. Hope will not disappoint.

When you need encouragement to keep going, when it's just so hard that you are tempted to give up, allow Christ to be the hope that keeps you going in the middle.

Father, thank You for the reminder that You are a God of hope. All things are possible with You. You are with me and for me. You have given me Your Son. All that is His is mine. Help me keep going, remaining faithful in the middle. Teach me to parent with great hope today. In Jesus' name, amen.

- Why is it often harder to be faithful in the middle than at the beginning?
- How can hope fuel your parenting or marriage?

the Real Value of Solitude

After [Jesus] had dismissed them, he went
up on a mountainside by himself to pray.
Later that night, he was there alone.
—MATTHEW 14:23

I am a doer, and nothing is more satisfying for a doer than being able to check things off a to-do list. While this trait enables me to accomplish a lot and stay focused, there is definitely a downside.

We live in a world that is all about doing. We crave productivity. Getting things done fast is important. We can begin to define our success by how productive we've been. Success is all too often defined as activity—doing. There's the danger for us.

If anyone ever had demands in life, if anyone was ever under pressure, under stress, or had a lot to do, it was Jesus. And yet when we look at Jesus' life, we notice that doing was not His only concern. In fact, we see that disengagement from people was just as important to Jesus' ministry as engagement.

Jesus often slipped away to be alone. He sought out solitude to pray. To commune with God the Father. He disengaged before starting His public ministry, before making important decisions, after intense ministry, and before going to the cross. Solitude was not just an option for Jesus; it was a necessary source of great strength.

Are you taking time to be alone? For all of the engaging you do as a mom, are you intentional about disengaging?

The real value of solitude is that we find strength in getting away and getting alone with God. He speaks to us. Fills us. Refuels us. A life lived for God needs to flow out of a life deeply rooted in Him.

Father, teach me the value of being alone with You. Help me be intentional about making space to draw near to You. Speak to me, and draw near to me. I want to root my life deeply in You as I seek to live a life for You. In Jesus' name, amen.

- What obstacles keep you from practicing the discipline of solitude?
- How can you begin to be intentional about making time for solitude?

Humility in Marriage

Do nothing out of selfish ambition or vain conceit. Rather, in humility value others above yourselves, not looking to your own interests but each of you to the interests of the others.

—PHILIPPIANS 2:3–4

We all struggle with the sin of pride. If we're honest, most of us live as if we're the center of the universe. And marriage doesn't take away our pride; marriage usually magnifies it. Our own selfishness becomes even more pronounced because we find ourselves bumping up against someone else's pride.

In order for Jesus to become greater in our marriages, we need to become less. In Christ, through the power of the Holy Spirit, God is working to cultivate in us the fruit of humility. Humility exchanges "me" for "you." Humility doesn't mean demeaning yourself; rather, it is choosing to elevate others.

As Paul wrote in today's verses, we aren't to be concerned about only our own needs and desires; we are to consider the needs and desires of others. Humility helps us to listen, be patient, and see our spouses' perspectives; to be quick to confess when we are wrong; and to sacrificially serve our spouses instead of our ourselves.

Has "selfish ambition" crept into your marriage? Is pride often at the center of your conflict? Then look at the example of Jesus, who came to sacrificially serve. Though He could have, Jesus did not live a "me-centered" life. Live humbly, as He did. Say no to your pride. Today, pray that God would give you an other-centered marriage. A marriage that is growing in humility instead of pride.

Father, forgive me for my pride and selfishness in marriage. Thank You for the example of Jesus, who came in humility to serve us and save us. Help me truly seek to serve my husband's needs and desires. Turn us away from ourselves, and turn us toward each other in love and humility. Give us grace to think less of ourselves and more of each other. In Jesus' name, amen.

- Where do you see selfish ambition at work in your marriage?
- What are specific ways you can look to the interests of your spouse? What is one way you can value your husband above yourself today?

The Changing Seasons of Motherhood

There is a time for everything, and a season
for every activity under the heavens.
—ECCLESIASTES 3:1

*E*very season of the year is different from the others, and the seasons of motherhood are no exception. We moms will have seasons of weeping and laughing, giving and receiving, planting and uprooting, speaking and being silent.

When our family of two became a family of three, my husband and I quickly discovered we were entering into a very different season of life. As our family grew, each child brought new joys but also new challenges. One of the most significant challenges for me was the realization that I couldn't do it all anymore!

I was working full-time. I was also involved in ministry at our local church, serving with my husband in a variety of ways. I was having an impact on my world, and I loved it. But with a growing family, my world was changing. Instead of late nights with teenagers from our student ministry, I was nurturing our kids. Instead of serving each week on our worship team, I was getting kids ready and hoping to make it to church on time!

Every family is different, and every season in a family's life together is different. But just because we move into different seasons, sometimes with limitations, doesn't mean we lose having an impact on our world. Living with limits doesn't meaning living less or having less of an impact.

So embrace the season you are in now. Don't be afraid to say no. Get creative about how you might engage in work or ministry during this unique season. Most of all, give yourself fully and wholly wherever you are. Each season is different but no less important. You can still have an impact on the world, no matter what season you are in!

Father, I know You have me exactly where You want me. Help me not to minimize this season, but to fully embrace it. Teach me where I need to guard my heart and family. I want to make the most of every season, using it to love You and love others. In Jesus' name, amen.

- What has been the biggest adjustment in this season of parenting?
- Are there things you need to say no to for now so you can embrace the season you are in?

Our Greatest Need

When Jesus saw their faith, he said to the paralyzed
man, "Son, your sins are forgiven." Now some
teachers of the law were sitting there, thinking to
themselves, "Why does this fellow talk like that? He's
blaspheming! Who can forgive sins but God alone?"
—MARK 2:5–7

What would you say your greatest need is right now? If you could
ask Jesus to do anything for you, what would it be? In Mark 2, we
discover that what we often ask Jesus for is not always what we actually
need most. This is what a paralyzed man and the four friends who low-
ered him through a roof to get to Jesus found out.

The people who had gathered to hear Jesus teach filled the house to
overflowing, so much so that the paralyzed man's friends couldn't get
him inside in the typical way—through the door. Instead, they had to
get up on the roof, make an opening, and lower him at Jesus' feet. We
don't read anything about Jesus' reaction to the damaged house; instead,
Jesus seemed less concerned about the house and more concerned about
the paralyzed man's needs.

Even more surprising is Jesus' diagnosis. You might expect Jesus to immediately heal the man of his inability to walk. But instead, Jesus' first words were, "Son, your sins are forgiven." This man went to Jesus for what he wanted, the ability to walk. But Jesus gave him what he needed most: a clean heart.

Our greatest need is the need to be forgiven. At the cross, Jesus made forgiveness possible, free, and final.

Have you gone to Jesus for what you need most? If so, are you continuing to allow Him, through the power of His Spirit, to help you turn from your sin? Pray boldly for healing. Keep asking in faith. Jesus came to give us life and life to the full.

Father, thank You for meeting my greatest need—forgiveness—at the cross. You want me to come to You for life; yet, I know my sin steals that life You offer. Search me and know me. Reveal the areas of my heart that need forgiveness and healing. And help me live as You would have me to. In Jesus' name, amen.

- What sin patterns have you noticed in your own heart?
- What sin do you need to ask God to forgive you for?

A Little Kindness Goes a Long Way

Dear children, let us not love with words or
speech but with actions and in truth.
—1 JOHN 3:18

I just needed a cup of coffee. It was going to be a long Saturday, full of soccer games, grocery shopping, and homework. As we sat in the drive-through of our local coffee shop, I was calculating how long it would be until I could devour my first cup of coffee of the day. Three cars ahead of us. Two cars. One car. Almost there.

When we finally pulled up to the window, the ten minutes of waiting in line evaporated with two short words from the barista as she handed me my coffee. As I reached for the coffee with my left hand and handed her my debit card with my right hand, she said, "You're good."

"I'm good?" I said, a bit confused.

"Yeah, someone paid for your drink. You're good. Have a nice day!" And a nice day I did have, thanks to an anonymous person's random act of kindness.

"Be kind to each other," Paul wrote in Ephesians 4:32 (NLT). Be "tender-hearted" to those around you. Do good. Be a blessing to the people you interact with. It's amazing to me how something as simple as a kind act can go a long way. It's a generous gift. Extend a compliment. Send an unexpected note. Make an encouraging phone call. Smile at strangers.

We live in a world where people all around us are carrying heavy burdens. People are hurting. Families are broken. God can use a simple act of kindness to spread His love. Who can you show kindness to today?

Lord, help me have eyes for others. Soften my heart for the people You put in my path. Change me by changing my focus. Give me opportunities today to live with a tender heart, showing kindness to those around me. In Jesus' name, amen.

- In what ways can God transform you by turning your attention to others?
- What is one way you can show kindness to someone today?

How to Be a Good Friend

"Do to others as you would have them do to you."
—LUKE 6:31

Several years ago I had a friendship "aha" moment. I had just gotten off the phone with a friend when I heard that quiet, sneaky voice in my head whisper, *Why didn't she ask how you're doing?* As that voice grew a little bit louder, my heart was growing a little bit harder. And then God's voice squashed that thought!

You see, it's so easy in friendships to want to find the perfect friend. The friend who always sends us encouraging notes, always asks how we are doing, always reaches out to us first, and always stops by unexpectedly with a gift or dinner. In fact, sometimes we can want the kind of friend we're not willing to be. And that was my "aha" moment, when God spoke loudly.

"Do to others," God reminded me. "Do to others" first what "you would have them do to you." In other words, I am to be the kind of friend I want my friends to be to me! It's tempting to wait for friends to take the first step. But Jesus reminds us to take the initiative: become the right kind of friend, and then receive such a friend.

What if we were more focused on being the right kind of friend first? How different could our friendships be if we spent time growing as a friend rather than waiting to find the perfect friend? Today, begin asking God to help you become the right kind of friend instead of looking for a perfect friend.

Father, thank You for loving me and saving me by faith in Jesus. I praise You for calling me a friend. You satisfy me and meet all of my needs. Give me grace with my friends. Shift my focus from finding friends to becoming the right kind of friend. In Jesus' name, amen.

- What makes someone a good friend?
- What is one step you can take today to serve or encourage another friend?

No Easy Route

Through laziness, the rafters sag; because
of idle hands, the house leaks.
—ECCLESIASTES 10:18

*L*et's be honest. We'd all like parenting to be a lot easier than it really is. But this messy mission is hard work. It's full of joy and pride, but it's also full of sweat and tears. Like a lot of truly important things, parenting comes at a cost. This is why when we feel overwhelmed, we have to be careful not to let laziness slip into our hearts and our homes.

Laziness has rightly been called a "silent killer" because it's not always easy to spot it in our own lives. Before we go further, let me be clear: laziness is not the same as rest. God definitely doesn't want us to run on empty. He created us for rest as well as work. In contrast to healthy downtime, laziness is that sneaky tendency to take the easy route. It's checking out when life's demands feel too overwhelming. It's cutting corners and compromising. At times, laziness is choosing the pleasure of serving ourselves instead of the pain of serving God.

The writer of Ecclesiastes observed that the "rafters" of our hearts and homes begin to sag when we check out of life. Everything we are building and all that God is working graciously through us to accomplish can "leak" when we routinely choose easy over hard.

We need to be diligent. Wise. Faithful. Willing to suffer and sacrifice.

God cares about our time. He cares about how we are using our days. He wants us to realize this window of opportunity will not remain open forever. Resist laziness at every corner. Ask God for His grace. Stay dependent on God for His grace, but give yourself diligently to the work He has set before you.

Father, thank You for my family. Thank You for the joy that comes with this calling. Forgive me for the times when I want this calling to be easier. Guard my heart from checking out or wanting to take the easy route. Fill me with Your Spirit so that I might avoid the dangers of laziness. Teach me to give myself fully, faithfully, and joyfully to my family. In Jesus' name, amen.

- Where have you been most tempted to be lazy as a mom?
- How do you balance work and rest?

Made Holy

We have been made holy through the sacrifice
of the body of Jesus Christ once for all.
—HEBREWS 10:10

*M*arriage is like a magnifying glass. In marriage, what gets magnified are our weaknesses, selfishness, and sinfulness. As we learn to share life and give life, we quickly discover we have a long way to go! Marriage humbles us and helps us grow in holiness. But holiness in marriage is not about our own effort; first and foremost, it is about what Jesus has done for us.

Holiness is a gift. Jesus died and rose again for us, giving us His holiness. So in the New Testament, we are encouraged to live up to what is already true of us in Christ. We have been forgiven, made pure and clean. Because Jesus has made us holy, we are now called to be holy. Being holy in marriage is no exception!

The word *holy* means "set apart." We are to guard the purity and sacredness of our marriages. We are to protect the intimate bond we have with our spouses, keeping the love we have for each other unblemished, spotless, and clean. We are called to "put off" our old lives (Ephesians 4:22), and crucify our sins. We are encouraged to have the "mind of Christ" (1 Corinthians 2:16). A healthy marriage is a holy marriage!

Today, remember what is already true of you in Christ. Because He has made you holy, pursue holiness. Ask the Father to show you areas where you need to be set apart from sin for the sake of your spouse.

Father, give me the desire to be holy. I know my husband and I cannot have a healthy and God-honoring marriage without pursuing holiness. Thank You for making me clean and pure in Christ. Now help me live set apart from sin so that I can continue to be set apart for my husband. Guard our marriage. Give us hearts that are broken over sin and that delight in doing what is pure, right, and true. In Jesus' name, amen.

- What area of your marriage needs the most growth?
- What is one step you can take with your spouse to pursue holiness?

Who Are You Working For?

Whether you eat or drink or whatever you
do, do it all for the glory of God.
—1 CORINTHIANS 10:31

God, among other things, is a worker. Work is the very first thing we find Him doing when we open the Bible. He was creating, cultivating, and commanding. He was working—and working hard.

Not only does God work, but He created us to work. For many of us as moms, that includes working from home, at home, or outside of the home. God created us to work, but not just work for ourselves.

We were created in God's image (Genesis 1:26–27). We were made like Him so others could get a good look at Him. In other words, our work isn't just for us. Our jobs aren't only about what we get from them. Our work has a greater purpose. And whatever God has given us to do—from changing diapers to running a Fortune 500 business—we are to do it for God's glory.

This is a difficult task at times, isn't it? Many people feel stuck in jobs they don't like. People get frustrated at times because of difficult coworkers or bosses. Others may like working, but their work doesn't always feel meaningful or appear to be fruitful.

Our work was never meant only to satisfy us. God created our work to be a means for showing others what He is like, but also as a means to serve others.

God wants to use your job for a greater purpose than paychecks, promotions, or personal fulfillment. God wants you to see your workplace, whatever it may be, as a mission field where He's placed you to serve, give, bless, and show others the love of Jesus.

Lord, I know that I am fearfully and wonderfully made. You created me to be in a relationship with You, but also to reflect who You are. Help me see that work is good, that You created it with a greater purpose than just what I get out of it. I want my work to be worship. Use my work to honor You and serve others. In Jesus' name, amen.

- Are there actions or attitudes you need to change in the workplace in order to serve others with your job?
- How can seeing your job as a mission change your perspective on work?

teaching Your Kids to Pray

"Our Father in heaven, hallowed be your name, your
kingdom come, your will be done, on earth as it is in heaven."
—MATTHEW 6:9–10

With four kids, my husband and I have heard prayers for just about anything you can imagine! We've prayed for sick hamsters, hurting neighbors, new bikes, and everything in between. While prayer is simply talking to God, there is a right way to talk to God. Even Jesus had to teach His disciples how to pray.

In Matthew 6, Jesus reminded the disciples that God is a Father, full of love and care. He not only sees us from heaven, but watches over us. He is a Father who is great and powerful. His name is to be "hallowed" or set apart. But in verses 9–10, we find an aspect of prayer that Jesus desires but is often missing in our prayers.

With "your kingdom come, your will be done, on earth," Jesus told His disciples to pray for a mission. He wanted them to pray for God's kingdom to come to earth. He wanted them to pray for more than just their own wants and needs. He was teaching them to pray for God to show up and have His way in their actions and everyday circumstances.

As a mom, I need this reminder. But I also want to begin teaching my kids to pray this way.

As we are raising kids who will one day grow up and love God and love the world, let's begin now to teach them to pray for a mission. Let's start teaching them to pray for God's will to be done in them and through them.

Father, thank You for Your love and goodness to me. I know that everything that comes into my life first comes through Your love. Help me pray with Your mission in mind and teach my kids to do the same. May Your reign and rule come through me today. In Jesus' name, amen.

- In what circumstances in your life do you need to be praying that God's kingdom would come and that His will would be done?
- What is one way you can begin teaching your kids to pray for God's kingdom to come and for His will to be done?

the One Who Judges Justly

When they hurled their insults at [Jesus], he did not
retaliate; when he suffered, he made no threats. Instead,
he entrusted himself to him who judges justly.

—1 PETER 2:23

We all like the idea of a loving God who is patient with us. In Christ, He forgives, redeems, and restores. He has set His affection on us like a parent loves his children. But what about a God who is Judge?

When the Bible describes God as Judge, it is describing God as a righteous King who governs, reigns, and defends His people. In His goodness, He is a Judge who promises to right all wrongs. As the psalmist declared, "The LORD is a God who avenges" (Psalm 94:1). Why is this such good news?

The good news is that God is not indifferent to the hurts we experience. Neither is He uninterested in the ways others have sinned against us.

If you have been hurt or wounded, know that God loves you. And because He loves you, He will not let sin go unpunished. Always the just Judge, He will take care of the wrong in His way and in His time.

Maybe someone has damaged your reputation. Perhaps you have

been treated unfairly. Whatever wrongs you have experienced, God has promised to make them right one day.

So let God be Judge. You and I don't have to try to punish or get even with those who hurt us. We can forgive and pray for them instead. We don't have to be the judge. Like Jesus, we can entrust ourselves to the One who judges justly and find the freedom to love and bless others.

Lord, You are King of all creation. I know that one day You will make right all wrongs. In the meantime, please guard my heart from anger and the desire to get even. Help me entrust myself to You, the One who judges justly. In Jesus' name, amen.

- How can the knowledge of God as Judge free you to forgive and love those people who have hurt you?
- Are you are trying to punish someone in your life? How can you entrust yourself today to the One who judges justly?

the Glory of Suffering

We also glory in our sufferings, because we
know that suffering produces perseverance;
perseverance, character; and character, hope.

—ROMANS 5:3–4

Several years ago I went through a period of about a year and a half
when the trials were numerous and the suffering was great. I felt as
if I would never be on the other side.

We've all gone through hard times we would rather have avoided.
The experience can leave us hardened and numb. But the truth is that
God uses our suffering to produce in us something beautiful and glorious. God uses our sufferings to make us better, transforming us into
who He created us to be.

What God is doing in us is far more important than what we are
doing for God. The apostle Paul wrote, "We . . . glory in our sufferings."
Most days I want to get out of my suffering, not "glory" in it! So why did
Paul say this? "Because we know that suffering produces" Christlikeness
in us. Through our struggles God shapes us, refines us, and molds us

more and more into the image of Jesus. Our suffering also has the potential to produce in us "perseverance . . . character; and . . . hope."

When Paul wrote about his own trials, he made it clear that they were not getting in the way of what God had for him. Paul's trials were hard, for sure, but they were no obstacle for God's power and purposes. Likewise, our suffering is not an interruption of what God is doing in our lives. Instead, our suffering may be the way God works in us and transforms us.

So how can you change your perspective of what you are going through right now to allow God to shape you? How can you see your season or circumstances differently, recognizing that what God wants to do in you is far more important?

Father, I know that You are using all of my life, including my trials, to make me more like Jesus. Help me cooperate with what You are doing in my life. Guard my heart against being hardened or indifferent. Grow me. Change all of me. Produce good things in my heart, even if the circumstances are hard. In Jesus' name, amen.

- What do you think it means to "glory" in your suffering?
- How can you change either an attitude or action that is related to your current circumstances?

Realistic Friendships

Always be humble and gentle. Be patient
with each other, making allowance for each
other's faults because of your love.
—EPHESIANS 4:2 NLT

I watched one of our neighbors walk past our house on the sidewalk. She lives just down the street and around the corner. This was the second time I saw her walk by. But she didn't walk all the way past. She stopped just where our sidewalk ends.

Between our house and the house next to us is an empty area where the builder has yet to finish the sidewalk. So between us, in this community space, are mud, rocks, and patches of mangled grass, which is probably why my neighbor stopped where the smooth, clean, and newly paved sidewalk ends.

On this particular day as I watched her from my upstairs window, it struck me that this is often how we approach friendships. We prefer the smooth and even pavement over the mud and rocks. We stay engaged in a relationship until it gets difficult, a little rocky, and more difficult to trek. Like my neighbor, we sometimes find it easier to turn around rather than to keep walking.

But the Bible doesn't paint a picture of easy friendships. Instead, we find pictures of real friendships, ones that have good days, but also really tough ones. In our friendships, we need to be realistic. Just as we are growing, so are our friends.

There is no perfect friendship other than the one Jesus offers us. So be a good friend. Don't expect your friends to be perfect. Thank God for the sidewalks in your friendships, and trust Him to give you grace to keep loving and giving, even when the sidewalk ends. As the apostle Paul instructed, "Be patient with each other." And be sure to give grace to people for their faults because of your love for them.

Father, guard my heart from expecting too much from my friendships. Help me make room for faults and imperfections. Teach me to love even when friendships aren't easy because this is how You love me. In Jesus' name, amen.

- In what ways can we idolize friendships?
- What is one thing you can do today to love a friend who is sometimes hard to love?

trusting God's truth

"Blessed are those who hunger and thirst for
righteousness, for they will be filled."
—MATTHEW 5:6

In the gospel of Matthew, we're told Jesus faced His share of opposition. In fact, when Jesus was led by the Spirit into the wilderness, He was immediately met with temptation. Three different times Satan tempted Him, twice saying, "If you are the Son of God . . ." (Matthew 4:3, 6).

But have you noticed how Jesus responded? He didn't try to argue with Satan, correct him, or explain things. Three times Jesus simply responded with a truth from Scripture: "It is written." In other words, Jesus' greatest defense was God's Word. It was so much a part of Him that at every turn, it just oozed out of Him.

What strengthened Jesus—what gave Him nourishment and sustenance—were the truth and promises of God's Word. He devoured the Word. Meditated on it. It brought strength and health when Jesus needed it the most. And God's Word can do the same for us.

We can get hungry as moms, can't we? We get hungry for friendships. We crave some peace and quiet. We can long for the way things used to be. But we must always remember that nothing satisfies and nourishes our souls like the truth of God's Word. More than how we are feeling, we need to remember what God says. His Word gives us hope, perspective, wisdom, and strength. God's Word is living and active, transforming us from the inside out.

Lord, thank You for the gift of Your Word. It is life. It is truth. It alone satisfies my soul. Help me cling to Your Word more than to my feelings or to people's opinions. Teach me to hide Your Word in my heart that I might not sin against You. In Jesus' name, amen.

- In what ways are you tempted to rely on how you feel instead of on God's Word?
- What is one thing you can do today to begin feeding on God's Word?

An Enemy of the Heart

A heart at peace gives life to the body,
but envy rots the bones.
—PROVERBS 14:30

We had no idea the freezer wasn't working. It had been months since we last put anything in or took anything out. So when we popped it open one evening to put some leftover meat inside, we were met with quite a surprise—a freezer full of rotting food. Yuck!

The Bible says that envy rots the bones. Like a freezer gone bad, envy creates an environment that spoils our hearts. Envy is sorrow over someone else's good fortune or blessing. At the same time, envy is the desire to have someone else's good favor.

If you've ever struggled to celebrate someone else's success, then you've struggled with envy. If you've compared yourself to others, feeling superior to them at times and inferior at other times, then you've struggled with envy. If you have ever secretly been resentful or bitter because of someone's marriage, parenting, or career, then you've struggled with envy.

It is true that a "heart at peace gives life to the body, but envy rots the bones." Contentment gives life; envy steals life. A great enemy of the heart, envy is always trying to draw our attention to what we don't have and what we wish we did.

Our best weapon against envy is gratitude. Our hearts are transformed when we focus on what we do have but don't deserve. We have been given all things in Christ (Romans 8:32), including forgiveness and eternal life. What more could we want? What more do we need? Yet God has also blessed us with family, friends, food, clothing, a place to live—and the list goes on.

A heart that is gripped by God's grace will be filled with good things like joy and peace, leaving no room for envy. What is your heart filled with today?

Father, thank You for blessing me beyond what I deserve. I praise and thank You for all that I do have but don't deserve. Guard my heart from envying the blessings You have given others. Fill my heart instead with gratitude and contentment because of all that You have given me. In Jesus' name, amen.

- When have you struggled to celebrate someone else's successes, especially that of other moms?
- What can you do today to focus on what you do have but don't deserve rather than what you don't have?

Speaking Life into Your Family

The tongue has the power of life and death,
and those who love it will eat its fruit.
—PROVERBS 18:21

*I*t's a sobering fact that our words reflect who we are. Jesus put it this way: "A good man brings good things out of the good stored up in his heart, and an evil man brings evil things out of the evil stored up in his heart. For the mouth speaks what the heart is full of" (Luke 6:45).

Clearly, ours is not simply a word problem; ours is a heart problem. Our words reveal what is going on in our hearts!

We use thousands of words every day—some suggest as many as ten thousand! The Bible teaches us that words are not neutral. Words carry weight and have significant power. I'm guessing you can still remember certain words that were spoken to you years ago. Some of those words were undoubtedly painful, but maybe others were positively powerful.

Words can make or break a marriage; they can make or break a child. Harsh, sarcastic, and controlling words can do indescribable damage.

But gentle, kind, and encouraging words can strengthen and protect a family.

Speak life into your marriage. Tell your husband you love him. Express your appreciation to him. Encourage him. Guard your lips from harsh or critical words.

Speak life into your children. Tell them often that you love them. Let them know the traits you appreciate that make them unique. Avoid harsh and critical words. Encourage your kids, and pray for them.

And ask God to change your heart so He changes your words. Pray that you would be cautious with not only what you say, but how you say it.

Father, help me be careful of how I speak to my family members. Renew my heart so that I might overflow with words that are loving, encouraging, and truthful. Guard my lips from tearing people down. I pray that You would strengthen my family by strengthening the way we talk to one another. Help me bring life, not death, to one another through the words we use. In Jesus' name, amen.

- What do you think your words reveal about your heart?
- What life-giving words will you speak to your spouse and your kids today?

Filling Your Home with Beauty

The LORD God had planted a garden in the east, in Eden.
—GENESIS 2:8

I have long envied the ability of an interior designer because I am the furthest thing from one. Especially early on in our marriage and family, I was just glad to have a house of our own. Who had the time, let alone the money, to decorate it? But as the years have gone by, I have learned the importance of filling our living spaces with greater purpose, beauty, and warmth. Much like God did in Eden at the very beginning.

When God first placed Adam and Eve in the garden, He didn't build them just any home. Eden was far from sterile or bland. Instead, with creativity, warmth, and beauty, He gave them a living space that would be a constant reminder of His goodness, power, and love.

God filled their living space with what was "pleasing to the eye" (Genesis 2:9). Color. Promises of life. Knowledge. It's no wonder God called the garden Eden, which means "delight"!

We don't have to have a big house or big budget to decorate our homes with beauty and reminders of who God is. We can paint walls to create rooms with warmth. Rearrange furniture to provide greater comfort and intimacy. Light candles. Open windows. Hang wall art or pictures with verses from God's Word. One of my favorites in our home is a large sign by the front door that reminds us as we leave to "Be the light."

You don't need to be an interior designer to make your home more comfortable and inviting. Simple reminders of God's beauty, truth, love, and power bring warmth to any home.

Father, thank You for the living space You have blessed me with. Help me transform my home into space that declares Your beauty, goodness, and truth. Fill it with Your presence, making our home a little sanctuary from the world for our family and friends. In Jesus' name, amen.

- How would you currently describe your living space?
- What are two ways you can fill your space with more beauty and warmth?

the Right Path

The LORD is my shepherd, I lack nothing. He makes
me lie down in green pastures, he leads me beside
quiet waters, he refreshes my soul. He guides me
along the right paths for his name's sake.

—PSALM 23:1–3

Recently my husband and I took up hiking. Several times a week we wake up early, just before the sun comes up, and drive to our favorite park. It's large and wooded, with steep trails, open meadows, and a river running through it.

At first I wasn't a big fan of hiking. I've always preferred the indoors over the outdoors! There were too many hills, loose rocks, and animals (or so I thought) lurking in the woods. As much as I preferred the predictability of a treadmill, though, I persisted in our new adventure.

The Bible talks a lot about paths, and walking is one of the most common metaphors used for describing a relationship with God. In Psalm 23, for instance, the psalmist said that God is like a shepherd who leads us down the right path. He lovingly invites us to follow Him into what is true and good, even if it looks like an uphill hike!

The path our good Shepherd has for us is not always an easy path. It's not always flat or free of obstacles. In fact, many paths God leads us down are thorny, steep, winding, and full of rocks. But if God is out front, that rugged path leads us toward life.

Still, in most of these rough spots, we'd choose a different way. One that was easier, shorter, and safer. The promise is never that the path will be smooth, but that the Shepherd will be with us. He knows what path is best for us.

No matter what kind of path you're on right now, remember you are not alone. So pray that regardless of the path, God would strengthen your legs and steady your feet, helping you trust Him on this journey of faith.

Father, lead me down the path that You have for me. Help me surrender to You and learn from You along the way. And when the path is hard, help me trust You. In Jesus' name, amen.

- In what ways do we often resist God's "right" path?
- How has God used a difficult path to change you?

the Power of Gentleness

A bruised reed he will not break, and a smoldering wick
he will not snuff out, till he has brought justice through
to victory. In his name the nations will put their hope.
—MATTHEW 12:20–21

Do your kids feel at ease in your home? Do they seem relaxed or on
edge? Sometimes in the stress and chaos of motherhood, we inad-
vertently create a home environment that feels more like a volcano on
the verge of erupting than it does an oasis for rest and refreshment. God
wants our homes to be sacred spaces, set apart to Him and for Him. How
we interact with family members is one way we can honor God with our
homes. Becoming better means looking to and learning from how Jesus
related to those around Him.

There's an interesting character trait of Jesus that often gets over-
looked. The gospel writers described Him as "gentle" (Matthew 11:29).
When Jesus interacted with people in His public ministry, He knew their
hearts and their brokenness. So Jesus was gentle with them. He wasn't
cynical, forceful, dismissive, rushed, or annoyed. Jesus interacted with
kindness and gentleness. He was careful not to break people's spirits.

Like Jesus, we need to be aware of any "bruised" reeds or "smoldering" wicks among our family members. Our homes should be a haven, a safe space away from all that is broken and wrong with the world. When we moms are gentle, we put our families at ease and make them feel comfortable. We de-escalate tensions instead of escalating them. We're patient. Gentleness helps us be compassionate—cautious with our words and intentional in our actions.

Lord, help me show my children the same kindness and gentleness You have shown me. Fill me with Your Spirit. Cultivate in me a heart that bears the fruit of gentleness so that I am more patient with my kids. Always help me remember that they are still growing and learning, just as I am. In Jesus' name, amen.

- Consider the ways each of your kids is like a "bruised reed" or a "smoldering wick." How could you be gentler with them?
- What might help you be gentler with your words?

God Hasn't Forgotten You

God remembered Noah.
—GENESIS 8:1

My husband and I have a running discussion about where the car keys should go. He is for the same spot: in a bowl next to our refrigerator. I, on the other hand, am for wherever is convenient when I come bursting through the door. Sometimes I put my keys on the kitchen table. Sometimes they go in my purse. Other times I stash them in my coat pocket. And a lot of times, well, I can't remember exactly where I placed them. We have this running discussion because I am prone to forget.

As I ponder my own forgetfulness, I am thankful for the reminder that God does not forget. The Bible tells us that Noah found favor in God's eyes (Genesis 6:8). When God told him to build an ark, he did it. We're told Noah did everything God commanded him to do (Genesis 7:5). Then the rain started to fall, and Noah's waiting began. God let rain fall for forty days and forty nights, and the earth was flooded for one hundred and fifty days, but we're told that "God remembered Noah."

I'm guessing Noah may have felt as if God had forgotten him and a boatload (literally) of animals. He must have thought, *Come on, God. Speed it up. What's taking so long? Where are You?* And then God "remembered." He kept His word.

Sometimes we can start to believe that somehow God has forgotten us. We wonder why He seems slow to answer our prayers or change our circumstances. We struggle to be patient. We doubt God's promises. We think He forgets.

If you feel forgotten today, know that God has not forgotten you. He remembered Noah, and He will remember you.

Father, I praise You for Your faithfulness. You are a God who keeps His promises. Even when I don't see You or feel You working, You are working to accomplish Your purposes in and through me. Thank You for the reminder that You will not forget me or forsake me. Help me cling to that promise today. In Jesus' name, amen.

- In what areas do you need to be reminded that God does not forget?
- What is one promise you need to cling to right now as a parent?

Love Anyway

"If you love those who love you, what reward will you get?"
—MATTHEW 5:46

*L*et's be honest. Sometimes we just don't see eye to eye with some people in our lives. Showing them love can be quite a challenge, especially when these people are difficult, different, or don't always show appreciation. But learning to love them anyway is a step closer to understanding the kind of love God has for us.

Have you ever thought about how out of balance our love relationship with God is? He first loved us, the Bible says (1 John 4:19). He made the first move and took the first step. By His grace, He sent Jesus for us to receive by faith. Our love in return, even on our best days, pales in comparison to that kind of love. Yet He loves us anyway. He doesn't give up on us when we don't give it back or show appreciation. In Christ, God loves us *anyway*.

As we begin to grasp just how wide and long and high and deep the love of Christ really is (Ephesians 3:18), we move closer to being able to love others in the same way God loves us. As we receive God's love and grow in His truth, God is producing in us a love that has the power to love anyway. And that kind of love is the greatest mark we can leave on the world!

So who is God calling you to love anyway? A friend who is difficult or different? A grumpy family member? A coworker who never seems to appreciate your efforts? Maybe it's your kids. As moms, we seem to always be giving and not necessarily getting much back in return.

Wherever we find hard-to-love people, may we open our hearts wide to receive God's love, and then may we be quick to share His love. May He empower us to love anyway!

Lord, I praise You for loving me first. Thank You for not giving up on me, even when I didn't love You back. Thank You for being patient, kind, and gentle. Pour Your love into my heart through Your Holy Spirit. Change me, and give me the power to love anyway. In Jesus' name, amen.

- Are there people around you right now whom you need to learn to love?
- What is one way you can love anyway right now?

Advice from a Friend

Listen to advice and accept discipline, and at the
end you will be counted among the wise.
—PROVERBS 19:20

We were sitting around the dining room table when the topic of dating came up. My friends' kids were at least ten years older than ours, and I was curious about how they had handled their kids' relationships with the opposite sex. "So what did you guys do that worked?" I asked. One question led to another . . . and then to another!

Do you have older friends who are great sources of advice? It might sound simple, but having wise moms in our lives and seeking out friends who are further down the road than we are is one of the best ways to learn to become better moms.

We need friends in all ages and stages of life. We need friends who are in the trenches with us. We have younger friends whom God has placed in our lives for us to mentor and encourage. And we also need older, wiser friends who will mentor and encourage us.

The writer of Proverbs instructed us to "listen to advice" and even accept "discipline." I am so grateful for older moms who have graciously poured their experiences and wisdom into me. I have learned so much from moms who led by example as well as from moms who were willing to listen and give advice, spurring me on in my calling as a mom.

The promise of this verse in Proverbs is that when we surround ourselves with wise people, we will be "counted among the wise" as well. Ask God to help you surround yourself with those who will raise the bar in your life, challenging you to grow better and wiser.

Lord, You have given me the gift of community for my benefit. Help me surround myself with friends who will spur me on to be better and wiser. Give me the humility to reach out to moms I respect. Help me be teachable for the sake of growing wiser and more like Christ. In Jesus' name, amen.

- Are most of your friends younger, the same age, or older than you?
- Where can you look for a godly mom who is older, further down the parenting path, and wiser because of her experience?

Source of Strength

Be filled with the Spirit.
—EPHESIANS 5:18

*N*othing reveals our limitations the way being a mom does. We quickly realize we don't have the resources to parent on our own. We don't just naturally become stronger and stronger so that we become better moms. This journey is about becoming weaker and weaker, realizing that God's power is made perfect in our weakness (2 Corinthians 12:8–9).

When we acknowledge our weakness, God gives us a very special gift: He gives us the gift of Himself. When we come to believe in Christ, God gives us His Spirit. This is why we are commanded to "be filled with the Spirit." We are to allow the Holy Spirit to lead us, teach us, and empower us. We weren't meant to live out this calling on our own. So how do we allow the Holy Spirit to fill us?

One of the best ways to be filled by the Spirit is by filling yourself with God's Word. God's Spirit works in many different ways. We might encounter God's Spirit through worship, through community, through times of prayer and solitude. But the surest and safest way to know we are encountering the Spirit of God is through the Book He inspired (2 Peter 1:20–21).

Are you spending time each day reading, meditating on, and memorizing God's Word? Are you trusting and relying on the truth and promises you find in its pages? When faced with difficult decisions or challenges, are you running to the Bible? If you don't, you're missing out on the strength God's Spirit wants to give you.

Whatever you are facing today, face it in the strength God is offering you. Be filled with His Spirit. Let your weakness cause you to run to His Word!

Father, You speak to me through Your Word, which is life and power. Fill me with Your Spirit today by filling me with Your life-changing love and truth. In my weakness, give me Your strength. In Jesus' name, amen.

- Why do you think it's so hard to admit to weaknesses?
- What can you do today to be filled with the Holy Spirit?

Fighting for Your Marriage

Be alert and of sober mind. Your enemy the devil prowls
around like a roaring lion looking for someone to
devour. Resist him, standing firm in the faith, because
you know that the family of believers throughout the
world is undergoing the same kind of sufferings.
—1 PETER 5:8–9

As much as marriage is a blessing, marriage is also a battle—and I don't mean spouse versus spouse! Having a healthy, God-honoring marriage requires fighting for each other. To be prepared for the battle, we need to remember who we are fighting so we know how to fight.

The Bible tells us on many occasions that we are really fighting against the devil, but being a deceiver, the devil doesn't always make his presence obvious. After all, our spiritual enemy disguised himself as a serpent in the garden of Eden when he targeted the first-ever marriage relationship. His assault brought sin, which resulted in separation, fear, blame, and shame. The oneness of marriage was under attack—and still is.

The enemy looks for vulnerable spots in a marriage. He looks for our weaknesses—those places in our walk with the Lord that are weak become opportunities for him to get a foothold. The best way to be protected is to be prepared, and that's why Peter told us we need to be alert. We need to have eyes to see real danger. Then we are to resist the devil by standing firm in our faith.

Be on your guard. Stay alert. Pray together. Pray with your spouse. Stay in God's Word. Surround yourselves with godly people and a church community. And keep your eyes on Jesus. He has given you the resources you need to fight for your marriage!

Father, protect my marriage. Give us spiritual eyes to see how some of our challenges or conflicts are really attacks from the enemy. Keep us prayerful, watchful, and saturated in Your truth. Jesus, You disarmed Satan's power at the cross. Your Spirit who lives inside of us is greater and more powerful than our enemy. Enable us to walk in Your power and victory. In Jesus' name, amen.

- In what part of your walk with the Lord are you most vulnerable?
- What is one thing you can do today to protect your marriage from spiritual attacks?

Walking with the Wise

Walk with the wise and become wise, for
a companion of fools suffers harm.
—PROVERBS 13:20

I'm not a "helicopter mom," but I am a protective mom. I freely admit that I shelter my kids. Not from everything, of course, but from a lot of things—especially from foolish friends.

As parents, we are the primary influence in our children's lives, but we are far from the only influence. As our children grow older, the influence of peers can, and usually does, grow greater. I know we can't protect our children from everything. I also understand that the sin inside of them (in their hearts) is just as real and dangerous as the sin outside of them (in the world). But there is great biblical wisdom in protecting our children from the wrong kind of friendships—a benefit they will take with them long after they are grown.

One of the things we can do as moms is give our kids a vision of godly friendship. While our kids don't come into the world knowing what Christlike friendships should look like, the Bible is full of examples of true friendship. A study in the book of Proverbs is a great way to give our kids a vision for choosing wise friends who bring blessing instead of suffering.

We can't protect our kids from every foolish friend, but we can prepare our kids to choose the right kind of friends. One effective way to teach our kids about godly friends is by letting them see our own friendships. In an increasingly disconnected society, our kids need to see healthy, loving, committed, self-sacrificial, and God-honoring friendships modeled before their eyes.

Father, give me wisdom to protect my children from the wrong kind of influences. I pray that You would bless my kids with friends who are pursuing Christ, friends who will love and encourage my kids in godliness. Use my kids to be positive influences on their friends, and help them pass on their faith in You to those around them. In Jesus' name, amen.

- In what ways have your children's friendships been a blessing? In what areas are you concerned for their friendships?
- What are a few things you can begin doing with your kids to help protect them from foolish friends?

Everyday Mission

Live such good lives among the pagans that, though
they accuse you of doing wrong, they may see your
good deeds and glorify God on the day he visits us.

—1 PETER 2:12

Since we moved to a new neighborhood last year, my husband and I have been intentional about taking walks. We wanted opportunities to talk to neighbors we hadn't met. We have been amazed at the conversations God has opened for us and the friendships that have already been formed. Through these simple walks, God has led to us to open our home and invite neighbors over for dinner.

Every day is full of ordinary opportunities to do something for God. Take a minute and think about all the daily activities you do, things like walking the dog, playing with your children, eating meals, working out, and going to the store. How can you use some of these everyday opportunities for God?

God wants to use each of us as moms in everyday, ordinary ways right where He has us in this season of life. Living on mission and influencing others can happen in our neighborhoods, workplaces, or homes or at our children's sports practices or coffee shops. The opportunities are truly endless.

In 1 Peter 2:12, we are reminded to live "such good lives" among our friends, family members, coworkers, and neighbors who don't know Jesus. There is something about our lives, our love, our families, or our marriages, that can put God on display for others to see. Our "good deeds" are good opportunities for non-Christians to see how good our God is.

Consider how you approach ordinary daily activities so God can use you. How can you live such a good life that others begin to see how good God is? Be intentional. Get creative. Take a risk. Then watch what God does!

Father, I want to live every day with purpose. This season of motherhood is unique and sometimes difficult, but I want to use it for You. Give me eyes to see how some of my ordinary and daily activities can be opportunities to influence others for Your glory. In Jesus' name, amen.

- What is one regular motherhood activity that you can transform into an opportunity to influence others?
- What are one or two good deeds that you or your family can do to put God on display?

Don't Waste the Wait

We wait in hope for the LORD; he is our help and our shield.
In him our hearts rejoice, for we trust in his holy name.
—PSALM 33:20–21

Have you ever noticed that there's a lot of waiting in the Bible? Abraham waited for an heir. Hannah waited for a child. King David waited for help. Israel waited for deliverance. But nobody likes to wait!

As human beings, we like things to happen fast. Today is better than tomorrow. So it's no surprise that some people in the Bible ran into trouble while they were waiting. Their waiting provided the perfect opportunity for their wandering.

Israel, fresh out of Egypt, is only one example. They had just seen the mighty hand of their Deliverer, experienced His gracious provision, and been blessed by His faithfulness. And yet, in a moment of waiting, they quickly wandered from God. In Exodus 32:8, we read, "They have been quick to turn away from what I commanded them and have made themselves an idol cast in the shape of a calf." I can't help but be struck by that phrase, *quick to turn away*. When God seemed slow to answer, they were quick to turn away.

How easily we can become discouraged, resentful, forgetful, impatient, and even disobedient when we're waiting on God. Maybe you're waiting for God's provision. Perhaps you are waiting for Him to right a wrong. Or maybe you are waiting for God to fulfill a promise. Regardless of your waiting, don't let it become an opportunity to wander. Be careful of being "quick to turn away." Wait for Him in hope. Turn to Him in trust. God never wastes our waiting.

Father, help me wait in hope. Guard my heart against wandering, doubt, or resentment. Help me trust You and wait patiently for You. I know that You are faithful, good, and present, even in the waiting. In Jesus' name, amen.

- In what situation are you waiting on God right now? What might your children be learning about waiting from your example?
- How do you "wait in hope"?

Friends Who Stay

Ruth replied, "Don't urge me to leave you or to turn back from you. Where you go I will go, and where you stay I will stay. Your people will be my people and your God my God."
—RUTH 1:16

I was sitting in a coffee shop recently when a woman sitting next to me struck up a conversation about change. I quickly learned that she hates it! She told me how much she disliked it when her favorite study spot rearranged the furniture and that she doesn't do well with changes at her job. Then she moved on to friendships. Some friendships in her past had fallen apart, and she informed me that I'd be lucky to find one or two friends who would stick around over the years.

Personally, I love change. But I couldn't agree more that good, faithful, stick-with-you kind of friends are hard to come by. Friendships that persevere, friends who love when times are hard, friends who are willing to forgive and reconcile when there is disagreement or conflict—those kinds of friendships are beautiful gifts.

The story from the book of Ruth is one of my favorites about friendships that stand the test of time. Ruth could have easily turned back and gone home. She was not obligated to follow Naomi. She was free to move on and start something new. But she stayed with Naomi. Ruth is a great example of a faithful friend.

In a culture where it is so easy to throw away one friendship for another, we need to be friends who are willing to stick with it. Especially during these messy parenting years when everything around us is changing, we need friends who don't! Let's strive to be the friend who loves unconditionally and remains committed no matter what. We can be the friend who stays.

Father, You are faithful. In Your love, You stick with me. You don't give up on me. Help me be the kind of friend who stays the course, loves, forgives, and offers hope to the friends You have placed in my life. In Jesus' name, amen.

- How has a friend blessed you by being willing to stick with you through the years?
- What is one way you can stick with a friendship that is hard right now?

Confessing Sin

If we claim to be without sin, we deceive ourselves
and the truth is not in us. If we confess our sins,
he is faithful and just and will forgive us our sins
and purify us from all unrighteousness.
—1 JOHN 1:8–9

Not too long ago, our Saturday morning breakfast turned into a discussion about which color our back deck should be. My husband wanted one color, I wanted another, and we both believed we had very convincing reasons for why we were right. Finally, I blurted out, "You are so stubborn!" To which my husband simply said, "No, I'm just right!"

Have you ever had one of those conversations? We joke about it now, but it's amazing that something so small and insignificant can turn into a conflict. Often at the heart of conflict is our own sin.

In the Bible sin is often described as separation. Our sin separates us from God and many times from one another. When we sin, our actions bring hurt into our relationships. This is why we need to be honest about our sin.

Being honest about our sin is acknowledging and admitting the pain our sin brings to our relationships. It is being alert to the ways our sin affects our desires, attitudes, thoughts, and behaviors—even silly conversations about the color of a deck! In marriage, we are not just two lovers, but two sinners sharing life.

Today, ask the Father to give you humility and grace. Seek the heart of God so that He will enable you to see your own sin, confess it, and chase after what He wants for you—which is always better for us than what we want for ourselves!

Father, I confess that I don't always do what You want in our marriage. I fall short, failing to live up to who You have called me to be. Give me grace. Help me look to Jesus for perfection and not my spouse. Teach me to walk in humility, being honest about my own sin. In Jesus' name, amen.

- How often do you confess your sin to your spouse?
- What is one way you can walk with greater humility in your marriage?

Every Marriage Needs Kindness

Be kind and compassionate to one another, forgiving
each other, just as in Christ God forgave you.

—EPHESIANS 4:32

What do you think of when you think of kindness? Would you use the word *kind* to describe your interactions with your husband? Kindness is a key ingredient for every life-giving, God-honoring marriage.

We honor God in our marriages when we treat our spouses the way He treats us. In Christ, God did not come with harsh and demanding words. Jesus came with kindness. The Bible encourages us to treat others in the same way Christ has treated us. We are to be "kind and compassionate" because that is how God acts toward us and because that's how we want to be treated.

Kindness is being gentle in how we talk (Proverbs 15:1). It's treating each other with respect. Kindness includes smiling at each other, encouraging each other, and being willing to forgive. In marriage, kindness is being concerned with our spouses' happiness more than our own.

How can you foster kindness in your marriage? What can you do to bring your husband joy with your words, attitude, and actions? "Be kind and compassionate to one another, forgiving each other, just as in Christ God forgave you." Allow God to cultivate in you a heart that is kind, gentle, compassionate, and forgiving. Ask the Father to help you be more concerned with your spouse's happiness than your own.

Father, help my husband and me treat each other tenderly, being careful of how we speak and act toward each other. Give us each a heart that really does want the best for the other. I pray that You would guard our lips and keep us from being harsh, critical, and sarcastic. Instead, may our words offer sincerity, respect, and kindness. Help us do for each other as You have done for us. In Jesus' name, amen.

- What prevents you from being kind to your spouse at times?
- What is one way you can bring happiness to your spouse?

Guarding Your Home

The LORD God took the man and put him in the
Garden of Eden to work it and take care of it.
—GENESIS 2:15

Do you remember what it felt like to be in your first home or apartment? A place that was just yours? Shortly after my husband and I were married, we settled into our first apartment in Chicago. It didn't take us long to begin making it feel like home. We bought new furniture. Painted the walls. Hung pictures. The apartment was tiny, cozy, and most importantly, ours.

A home is sacred space. It's not only a place where we live, but also a place where God's presence dwells.

When we open the Bible, one of the first stories we read is about God giving Adam and Eve a place to live. That place was the garden of Eden. Adam and Eve would not just live in Eden; they were "to work it and take care of it." This charge was far more important than rearranging furniture and decorating walls!

When God told the first couple to work and take care of their home, He was telling them to guard it. It wouldn't take long for Satan, disguised as a serpent, to make his way toward their home. With evil lurking, the command to guard their home was too important to ignore.

Just as He did in Eden, God wants our homes to be places where His Word is honored and His will is obeyed. As we cultivate our marriages and grow families, God's Word is an important reminder for us. How are we guarding our homes and our hearts? Where do we need the reminder to watch over what matters most?

Father, I know that You have not called me to be fearful of our enemy, but You have called me to be wise. Your Word commands me to be watchful. Help me be watchful over my marriage and family. May my home be a place where You are honored and evil is pushed back. In Jesus' name, amen.

- What are common ways Satan attacks a home?
- What are several ways you can guard your heart and home?

God Works with What You Have

[David] took his staff in his hand, chose five smooth stones
from the stream, put them in the pouch of his shepherd's bag
and, with his sling in his hand, approached the Philistine.

—1 SAMUEL 17:40

Not a single soldier in Israel's army wanted to go out and fight the Philistine named Goliath. For forty days this giant of a man taunted . . . waited . . . heckled . . . and essentially mocked the entire army until one Israelite had had enough. Young David was going to fight Goliath. Not alone, but with God.

A shepherd boy, David wasn't even supposed to be on the battlefield. But when he heard Goliath taunting God's army, he couldn't take it anymore. Israel's king, Saul, offered David his own armor, which the Bible tells us just didn't feel right. Off it went. Instead, David gathered what he had. Five smooth stones. A shepherd's bag. His sling. And the God of Israel.

The rest is history. Goliath was no match for David—or rather,

David's God. The Lord Almighty had given His people victory, and it came at the hands of a young shepherd boy who was willing to step out in faith and allow God to use what he had.

Isn't that the way God always works? God uses what we have, not what we wish we had. For David, it was five smooth stones. For Moses, it was a staff. Gideon had a torch and some jars.

The Lord uses your gifts, not someone else's. He uses your experiences and your past. He takes what feels like scraps of fish and bread, and He multiplies them. This is the way God has always worked and is working with you. He wants to use what you do have and not what you wish you had.

Father, this is Your work. It's not about me. Would You take what I have and use it to help shape my kids? Would You work in me, with what I have, to do great things in my family? In faith, I am trusting You today. In Jesus' name, amen.

- In this daunting task of parenting, why do you sometimes focus on what you don't have instead of what you do have?
- In what aspect of your life do you need the reminder that God will use what He's given you to help you tackle the challenges you face?

Sharpen the Mind

"Love the Lord your God with all of your heart and
with all your soul and with all your mind."
—MATTHEW 22:37

We were sitting around our community pool when our son's friend said to him, "You've never heard of the Big Bang? You know, like how the world began?" I'm not sure how the topic came up, but the boys' conversation got deep fast.

As I listened, I was struck with how important it is for us moms to prayerfully help shape our kids' minds and prepare them to face tough topics and hard conversations. Now is the time to help them know not only what they believe, but also why they believe it (1 Peter 3:15).

Like a farmer planting seeds, we have the joy and responsibility of planting the truth of God's Word in our children's hearts when they're young and thinking more concretely. Those seeds will bear fruit in the years to come. But as our kids grow older, they will begin to think more abstractly. They will want and need explanations about why they believe what they believe.

So be patient with your kids, and give them permission to ask hard questions. When they are tweens and teens, begin giving them age-appropriate books or videos on why the Christian faith is reasonable. As moms, we are not to pressure our kids to choose to follow Christ, but we can prepare them to want to choose Christ. Begin now, helping them learn to love God with all of their hearts, with all of their souls, and with all of their minds.

Lord, help me be intentional about training my children to grow up to love You with all of their hearts, souls, and minds. Give me the wisdom and the resources to shepherd them in this way. I pray that You would guard their minds from the enemy's lies and allow the truth of Your Word to take root and grow, producing in them a harvest of righteousness. In Jesus' name, amen.

- What is the difference between *pressuring* a child to follow Jesus and *preparing* a child to follow Jesus?
- What are some age-appropriate ways you can help your children not only know what to believe, but know why to believe it?

Clothed in Humility

All of you, clothe yourselves with humility
toward one another, because, "God opposes the
proud but shows favor to the humble."
—1 PETER 5:5

We were hustling around the house, running late, of course, for the kids' first day at our new homeschool co-op. Suddenly our youngest and most fashion-savvy son, Noah, appeared in the family room. He was decked out in black and red high-top basketball shoes, grey camo joggers, and a blue and orange Denver Broncos jersey. It was a collision of colors! Much to his dismay, I had to inform him that his outfit really didn't work, and he needed to change a few things.

The Bible often talks about transformation and growth like a change of clothes. When we come to know Christ and desire to grow in Him, we are called to take off certain clothing and put on new clothing. First Peter 5:5, for instance, tells us to "clothe" ourselves with humility. We are to dress each day, in attitude and action, with humility. Paul gave this instruction: "In humility, value others above yourselves, not looking to your own interests but each of you to the interests of the others" (Philippians 2:3–4).

Pride is always turned inward; humility is turned outward. Pride is me-centered; humility is others-centered. One of the ways that God uses parenting is to help teach us to look beyond our own interests, and instead help us to focus on the interests of others.

Consider what "clothing" you might need to change, what character qualities might you need to "take off," so that you can put on humility. Accept God's call to focus more on others and less on yourself. Clothe yourself in humility. Doing so will help you love God and love others well!

Father, teach me to walk in humility. Clothe me with a sincere and sacrificial love for others. Enable me to be less preoccupied with myself and to be more focused on You. Give me the attitude of Jesus, who lived to love and serve others. In Jesus' name, amen.

- In what ways is pride most dangerous to your parenting right now?
- Rick Warren said, "Humility is not thinking less of yourself; it is thinking of yourself less."[3] How can you practice self-forgetfulness today?

Looking Beneath the Surface

"If you knew the gift of God and who it is that
asks you for a drink, you would have asked him
and he would have given you living water."
—JOHN 4:10

Friends who truly know us pay attention and see things in us that other people don't. They notice when we are doing well and when we seem to be running on empty. Friendships that fuel our souls are friendships with vision. We all need friends who see clearly.

Have you noticed how often we read in the gospels that Jesus "saw" people? Jesus was good at noticing, and He was good at seeing. He was a friend of sinners; He saw people, loved them, and moved toward them with compassion.

Jesus saw His first disciples standing along the sea (Matthew 4:18). Jesus saw Peter's mother-in-law lying sick in bed (Matthew 8:14). Jesus saw the multitudes hungry and was moved with compassion (Mark 6:34). He noticed the sick woman and set her free (Luke 13:12). Jesus saw that the rich man's idol was his money, and He was filled with sorrow (Luke 18:24).

Jesus is a great example of the kind of friend we need and the kind of friend we need to be.

The gift of other people is that they know us. They love us enough to sometimes even confront us in grace and truth. A community of faith in which people are pursuing Christ is a beautiful gift because they delight in honoring God more than in keeping us happy at times. I love how Henri Nouwen described the role of Christian friends: "It is far from easy to keep living where God is. Therefore, God gives you people who help to hold you in that place and call you back to it every time you wander off."[4]

We all need friends with vision. We need friends who know us, love us, and see when we need to be encouraged, challenged, and even held accountable. We all need the gift of friends who hold us in that place of walking with God and call us back to Jesus when we wander, grow weary, or feel alone.

Father, thank You for keeping Your eyes always on me. You know me, love me, and see me. Help me have eyes to see those around me. Give me wisdom to pay attention to other moms who might be struggling. And bless me with the gift of friends who see me, care about me, and support me. In Jesus' name, amen.

- Why do you need friends who not only love you, but who love you enough to tell you the truth about yourself?
- What is one thing you can do to be a friend who pays attention?

Staying Power

Let us run with perseverance the race marked out for us.
—HEBREWS 12:1

*B*eing a mom is not a jog in the park, is it? It's easy to get tired. Worn out. Both the Christian life in general and parenthood in particular are much more like a marathon than a leisurely jog. Each is a grueling run, not a quick sprint. Each is full of twists and turns, ups and downs. And like any lengthy and challenging journey, parenthood is full of moments when we want to throw in the towel!

That's one reason I love the reminder from the writer of Hebrews that this calling we are all chasing requires perseverance. We are to stay in the race, enduring when we're bone tired and emotionally spent, patiently and steadfastly working to fulfill our purpose to raise kids who will one day grow up to love Jesus and love the world. In other words, this isn't an easy assignment. The truly meaningful things rarely are. We can't afford to be easily swayed. We are to "run with perseverance."

We are told not only to run a race, but to run the race God has marked out for us. Not the race of a neighbor, friend in Bible study, coworker, mentor, favorite blogger, pastor, or friend. We are to run the race Jesus has marked out for each of us. Run the race marked out for you!

By fixing our eyes on Jesus, we stay faithful to the course He has for us. The promise for those who persevere is that, in time, we will reap a harvest. We will see the fruit of our labor (Galatians 6:9).

So don't give up. Keep going. By God's grace, keep persevering as a parent. It will be worth it!

Father, give me grace today. Fill me with Your strength. Renew my faith, my energy, my focus. Help me stay the course, running this parenting journey with patience and perspective. Remind me to run my race faithfully, knowing that You are with me, supplying all of my needs every step of the way. In Jesus' name, amen.

- Where are you most weary as a mom right now?
- When have you been tempted to run someone else's race?

Looking at the Cross and Beyond

Worthy is the Lamb, who was slain, to receive
power and wealth and wisdom and strength
and honor and glory and praise!
—REVELATION 5:12

Nearly every room and every wall of my childhood friend's house had a cross on display for everyone to look at. Since I wasn't a Christian at the time, I didn't think much of it. I've now spent twenty-five years following Jesus. We don't have crosses hanging on every wall of our home. But over the years I have spent much time looking at the cross. Admiring it. Meditating on it. Thanking God for all that He accomplished through it. Rejoicing that my sins were dealt with on it.

On the cross Jesus was crucified for my sin. He took my place for the punishment I deserved. His shame covered my sin. Instead of God's wrath, I now drink of God's love. But I am also learning not to stop at the cross.

One of Jesus' earliest followers was a great example of not only looking at the cross, but looking beyond it—to see Jesus as He is now.

When Jesus hung on the cross, the disciple John saw Jesus as He was. John was "standing nearby" (John 19:26) as Christ died for the sins of the world. And then we're told that John, much later in his life, was given a vision of Jesus as He is now, the exalted and reigning King.

What a great reminder to look not only to the cross, but to look to heaven's throne. Jesus was crucified, buried, and raised to life, and now He is reigning as King of kings. He is alive. Ruling in power. Sovereign over all creation. Worthy of our praise. Deserving of our trust. Returning soon.

We need to look to the cross, but we also need to look beyond it to heaven's throne.

Father, thank You for the cross. Lift my eyes today to see Jesus as He is. In control. Ruling. All powerful. And soon returning. In His powerful and beautiful name, amen.

- Why is it important to look at both the cross and the throne?
- How does looking from the cross to the throne enable you to live more freely and joyfully as a mom?

A Heart of Praise

Let everything that has breath praise the LORD. Praise the LORD.
—PSALM 150:6

Have you ever noticed that the book of Psalms ends with praise? Psalms was the prayer book for the nation of Israel. This collection of heartfelt lyrics contains cries of anguish, pleas for help, honest questions, petitions for justice, and declarations of faith. The songs reflect what most of us would pray in private but dare not sing—especially not in front of other people!

I love the writers of the psalms for their realness. Their words remind us that we're all flawed, yet we can all come to God. We come messy, hurting, questioning, tired, and waiting. God is okay when we come to Him with it all.

And then praise. Finally, praise. The last five chapters of the Psalms are filled with praise. They serve as a great reminder that no matter how we come to God, when we truly encounter His love, we can't help but leave Him with praise. All of the messiness, pain, and waiting gets swallowed by a chorus of "Praise the LORD"!

Let's start today with where all of history will end—in an attitude and spirit of praise! Don't go through today focusing on what you don't have or what you wish you had done. Lift your eyes to see all that is yours in Christ. In both your heart and your home, lift Jesus up in praise for all that He has done, is doing, and will do one day.

Lord, You are worthy of all praise. You are powerful, good, wise, faithful, and loving. There is no one like You. Lord, help me lift my eyes above my circumstances and my emotions and see You for who You really are and all that You have done. Fill my heart with praise today as I shepherd my children and love my family. In Jesus' name, amen.

- Some people hide their emotions. Other people seem to be slaves to their emotions. Why is it so important to take your emotions—both good and bad—to God?
- How can the way the book of Psalms ends in praise encourage you as a mom?

the Gift of Being Known

"What do you want me to do for you?"
—LUKE 18:41

I love to talk. Just ask my husband! Words come easily to me. And often.

That being the case, one of the things I love about the opening chapters of the Bible is the fact that God speaks too. God spoke, and creation happened. He brought forth light, life, beauty, and order. Lately, however, I've been noticing how often God and His Son asked questions.

God asked Adam, "Where are you?" (Genesis 3:9). He asked Cain, "Where is your brother?" (Genesis 4:9). Jesus asked Peter, "Who do you say I am?" (Matthew 16:15). And when encountering a blind man in Jericho, Jesus compassionately asked him, "What do you want me to do for you?" (Luke 18:41).

God asks questions like these because He cares. He asks questions and invites conversation for our sakes. Questions bring discovery, intimacy, and many times, needed change. The truth is, many of us are far better at talking than we are at asking questions.

Maybe that's why it can sometimes be easy to be together, to be in community, yet never get beneath the surface. Our talk can get in the way of the truth about challenges, fears, pressures, and heartaches hidden in our hearts.

Questions are a rare gift to a friendship. When we ask a friend a question, we give her the opportunity to be known: *How are you doing today? What are you struggling with most right now? What are you most excited about? How can I be praying for you? What's going on in your marriage or family? What kind of work is God doing in your heart lately?*

Be a friend who is willing to give the gift of being known. Don't settle for just talking. Be intentional about asking questions. It is a rare but necessary gift that we all need to grow in as we become more and more like Christ.

Father, help me be a different kind of friend—a friend who intentionally asks questions. Create in me a heart that loves the people around me and shows my love by noticing, asking, listening, and speaking words of wisdom, truth, and encouragement. In Jesus' name, amen.

- Why do we tend not to ask questions?
- What do you need to change in order to be a friend who asks questions?

You Are Invited

"Come, all you who are thirsty, come to the waters; and
you who have no money, come, buy and eat! Come,
buy wine and milk without money and without cost."
—ISAIAH 55:1

What do you really believe will satisfy you? What is it, right now,
that you think about? What, if you had it, would make you happy?
The Bible uses the language of drink and food to describe our deepest longings. We do get physically hungry and thirsty, but the thirst and
hunger Isaiah referred to are metaphors for what our souls really need.
This language of drinking and eating is meant to point us to what will
truly satisfy, strengthen, comfort, and fulfill us.

Four times in Isaiah 55:1, we see God's gracious invitation to "come."
Those who are thirsty, "come" to the source of living water. Those who
have no money and are hungry, "come" and be filled at no cost.

Israel as a nation had wandered from their God. They had gone
looking for joy, satisfaction and pleasure in other places. Like all of our
own misplaced pursuits, the Israelites had taken their thirst and hunger
elsewhere and come up empty. Apart from God, they felt the void. The

emptiness. Brokenness. Because there is only one Source that satisfies the soul.

In John 4:10, Jesus said we are to come to Him, and we will find our thirst quenched. He is living water. Jesus' invitation is still open. God is still asking. Will you "come"? Will you have your deepest thirst and hunger met by Him?

Come find God in His Word. Come to Him in prayer. Kneel before Him in humility. Get alone to hear His voice. Today, right now, Jesus is inviting you to come to Him to be satisfied.

Father, only You can satisfy my soul. Forgive me for turning to other sources too soon or too often. Thank You for your gracious invitation to "come." I come to You today. Fill me. Comfort me. Satisfy my deepest thirst and hunger. In Jesus' name, amen.

- Where do you look to find comfort or satisfaction?
- What is one thing you can do today to find your satisfaction in Him?

Pursuing Wisdom

The fear of the LORD is the beginning of knowledge,
but fools despise wisdom and instruction.
—PROVERBS 1:7

After twenty years of marriage I can confidently say that there was not enough premarital counseling in the world to prepare Patrick and me for all the different and difficult circumstances we have encountered thus far! We don't enter marriage—or life, for that matter—with everything figured out. That's why we need wisdom. And lots of it!

The Bible presents two ways to live: wisely or foolishly. One way leads to life; the other leads to death. Wisdom, which is the path to life, is really skilled living. It is knowing and applying God's truth to whatever comes along in our lives so that God is glorified and we experience love, joy, peace, patience, kindness, goodness, faithfulness, gentleness, and self-control (Galatians 5:22–23). These are all fruits of the Spirit-filled and Spirit-empowered life.

With all of the everyday decisions, circumstances, stresses, and challenges, husbands and wives need to seek God's wisdom. The good news is that the Bible says when we lack wisdom we should ask God, who gives wisdom "generously" (James 1:5). When we seek wisdom by reading the Bible, God gives it. When we search for wisdom in prayer, God gives it. As we seek godly counsel, God graciously and generously gives us what we need to live in a way that honors Him.

Today, pray that God would give you and your spouse wisdom. Wisdom to know and understand the truth. Wisdom to make godly decisions. Wisdom to walk in righteousness. Wisdom for parenting. Wisdom with finances. Wisdom to love and serve each other well. And wisdom about how to glorify Him in your marriage.

Father, I want You to be at the center of my marriage. Help us revere You as a couple. Give us a heart of wisdom that we might know You and live well in a culture that is lost and broken. Keep our steps far from the path of foolishness. With all of the different decisions and circumstances we find ourselves in, give us wisdom to do what is right. We want to please You and honor You. In Jesus' name, amen.

- Where do you need God's wisdom most right now?
- What is one way you can pursue wisdom today?

A Song-Filled Home

The LORD your God is with you, the Mighty Warrior who
saves. He will take great delight in you; in his love he will no
longer rebuke you, but will rejoice over you with singing.

—ZEPHANIAH 3:17

*S*ing to me one more time, Mommy," my daughter said.

From the time our kids were born, I found it easy and natural
to sing over them. Tucking them into bed, I'd sing "Jesus Loves Me," "The
B-I-B-L-E," and "Jesus Loves the Little Children." Each of our kids loved
to sing when they were young, which is why every last song was always
followed with, "One more time, Mommy!"

There is something about music and singing that soothes the soul.
And not just at bedtime. Music can soften a hard heart, quiet our fears,
give us hope, and remind us of God's truth. In a home, music can change
the tone or help create an environment for thanksgiving, joy, laughter,
and fun.

Over the years we have intentionally turned on music in our home.
We play worship songs from an iPad or phone. We add worship music to

family devotions. And even though my kids are getting older, they still occasionally ask me to sing with and to them.

Are you filling your home and your kids' hearts with song? The Bible tells us that we are not the only ones who sing. Like a father or mother, the God who created us sings to us and over us with love, affection, and approval. Let's do the same for our families and in our homes.

Father, thank You for rejoicing in me. Thank You that because of Jesus, I am forgiven and loved. Help me create a home that is filled with praise and gratitude. Use my home as a sacred space. Fill my home and my heart with songs of love, truth, and praise for all that You have done. In Jesus' name, amen.

- How has music had the biggest impact on you spiritually?
- What are a few simple ways you can add music and singing to your home?

What Not to Say to God

Moses said, "Pardon your servant, Lord.
Please send someone else."
—EXODUS 4:13

I can empathize with Moses. I don't blame him for feeling a little overwhelmed and unqualified to go to Egypt. God commanded Moses to go to Pharaoh and tell him to let the enslaved Israelites go. The assignment seemed simple enough, except for the fact that Pharaoh was the leader of the most powerful empire on the planet. And Moses? He was a runaway Hebrew, a shepherd.

But God promised Moses that He would go with him (Exodus 3:12). You would think that would be enough to satisfy Moses, but it didn't. After a little more back-and-forth with God, Moses came up with the excuse that he wasn't gifted enough for the job. "I am slow of speech and tongue," Moses explained to God (Exodus 4:10). That didn't get Moses out of the mission either.

Finally, Moses made the biggest mistake of all. He suggested sending someone else! Exodus 4:13 records his words, "Pardon your servant, Lord. Please send someone else." Up to this point, the Lord had been gracious and patient with Moses. God had reassured Moses with His presence and strength. But Moses' last request changed everything.

Exodus 4:14 says the "LORD's anger burned against Moses." It wasn't until Moses tried to sidestep something God wanted him to do that God grew angry. As the story unfolds in Exodus, Moses did go to Pharaoh, and God worked powerfully through Moses to deliver the Israelites from slavery in Egypt. But don't miss the importance of God's reaction to Moses' attempt to get out of going!

Is God calling you to do something that you feel unqualified to do? Learn from Moses' experience. Trust that you are exactly where God wants you! Don't tell God to send someone else to do what He has called you to do.

Father, I know that You love and accept me because of what Jesus has done for me. I want to honor You in all that I do, even when I feel as if the task is too big. Show me areas where I'm resisting Your call on my life, and give me strength to obey You. In Jesus' name, amen.

- In what area of your life do you feel overwhelmed by what God is calling you to do?
- How is the story of Moses an encouragement to you?

A Twist on Holiday Giving

Command them to do good, to be rich in good
deeds, and to be generous and willing to share.
—1 TIMOTHY 6:18

*L*iving on mission doesn't have to be complicated. Each day is filled with ordinary opportunities to love and serve those around us. But the holidays are also a great opportunity for our families to have an impact on the world in simple, tangible ways.

I love what my in-laws used to do every Christmas. Instead of buying presents for one another, each family member would donate a certain amount of money. Then they would give it to a family, a widow, a college student, or a neighbor—someone they knew who was in need. This was a practical and powerful way for their family to share the love of Christ with others around the holidays.

Our world is full of opportunities for us to do good, and we are commanded "to be rich in good deeds, and to be generous and willing to share." The holidays are a great time of the year to intentionally reach out to friends, coworkers, neighbors, or someone from church who is in need. We don't have to travel the globe to have an impact on the world.

Hurting people all around us are waiting to hear about the God who loves them and to experience the hope of Christ.

Think about what good you and your family can do together. Is there something you can do without so that you can help someone else? Get creative. Be generous. Do good. And just see what God does with one simple act of obedience!

Father, You have given me far more than I deserve. Thank You for Your rich blessings in my life. You have saved me, forgiven me, and given me hope and peace. You have been so generous to me. Help me see my world differently. Give our family an opportunity to do good, be generous, and show Your love in a practical and tangible way. In Jesus' name, amen.

- What is one idea you have to bless someone else over the next holiday?
- What can you begin doing without right now in order to be generous to someone else?

Choosing Patience

Love is patient.
—1 CORINTHIANS 13:4

*P*atience and parenting sometimes feel about as compatible as oil and water. As moms, it feels as if we are always hurrying somewhere and hurrying someone. Our impatience, though, reveals far more about our hearts than our hurried lives.

I've found that my impatience is often a reflection of my own selfishness. I get upset and impatient when things don't go my way. It creeps in when nothing is going smoothly or as planned—and it's evidence of a me-centered life. Thankfully, the new heart God is creating in us through the Holy Spirit is marked by patience (Galatians 5:22).

But the real reason we are to be patient with our kids is because God is patient with us. As much as we hurry in motherhood, God is in no hurry with us.

The Bible describes God as patient: "The LORD is compassionate and gracious, slow to anger, abounding in love" (Psalm 103:8). God was not only patient for you to come to Him, but He is also patient for you to grow up in Him. The apostle Paul said that's what true love is: "Love is patient." It takes its time. It slows down. It waits. God's love is patient, not pushy.

In faith, be patient today, trusting that God is at work even when things don't go the way you want. And be reminded that God is not in a hurry with you. He, in His love, is patiently and persistently changing you from the inside out. He takes joy in you, knowing that the work He started in you will be brought to completion.

Lord, You are slow to anger and abounding in love. Thank You for being patient with me and for allowing me time to grow. Help me be a mom who reflects Your patience to my kids, showing them the kind of love You have for each of them. In Jesus' name, amen.

- How can God's patience with you help you to be more patient with your kids?
- How can knowing that God is patient with you be an encouragement in your spiritual growth?

God Is with You

The Word became flesh and made his dwelling among us. We have seen his glory, the glory of the one and only Son, who came from the Father, full of grace and truth.

—JOHN 1:14

There we were, standing in the Home Depot parking lot and staring at the van. Then we turned and stared at the stack of lawn chairs we had just purchased. I was doing the calculations in my head. It was going to take a miracle for this big stack of chairs to fit into our van! How could something so large be corralled into such a tight space? I always seem to underestimate the space needed to fit such purchases in the car, but believe it or not, we made it work.

In many ways, this is the story of God coming to us in Jesus. The disciple John wrote that "the Word became flesh." The greatness and bigness of God the Son squeezed into time and space and a human body. That's a far greater miracle than managing to get a massive stack of lawn chairs packed into a minivan. The glory and power of God are beyond measure, yet He humbly chose to become small enough to come to us.

I love this reminder. I need this reminder. My children do too. God is not so big that He would ever forget us. God was and is and always will be with us. While God is holy and great beyond imagination, He made Himself small. He came near us to love us, to save us, and to allow us to know Him more deeply. No need or concern is too small to take to God. From start (Matthew 1:23) to finish (Matthew 28:20), Jesus is God with us. He has not, and He will not, leave us. He is big, but not so big that He would ever forget us.

Lord, You are worthy of all of my praise. You are King of kings and Lord of lords. There is no one like You. And yet You care about me. You know me. Thank You for not being too big to forget about me. In Jesus' name, amen.

- Where do you need the reminder that God is not so big that He will forget you?
- What are one or two ways you can help your children to know that God will not forget them?

When Anxiety Is Overwhelming

When anxiety was great within me, your
consolation brought me joy.
—PSALM 94:19

It's comforting to me to know that many of the men and women of faith in the Bible wrestled with fear. "Anxiety was great" within them, just as it can be within me.

As moms, we know exactly what it means to console a frightened or anxious child. Sometimes the anxiety is for good reason: a child is overwhelmed with homework or is worried about making new friends. Other times the anxiety is unwarranted, such as a fear of the dark. Whatever fuels it, the anxiety can feel "great" within our kids, just as it can within us. So as a mom who has experienced anxiety, you know what it means to console. Your calming, reassuring, and encouraging words and presence brings comfort where there is anxiety.

I love Psalm 94:19 because it reminds me we have a Father who offers His consolation to us. He replaces our anxiety with joy. He quiets our fears with His presence. He whispers to us His words of truth and encourages us with His faithful promises. And most of all, He gently turns our eyes back to His own Son, as if to say, "I didn't forsake Him; I won't forsake you. If you are in Him, I am with you."

Is anxiety great within you today? Do your circumstances seem impossible? Does the future seem overwhelming? Has fear stifled your faith, stopping you in your tracks? Whatever you're facing today, be encouraged that in Christ, God is with you. You have a Father who is good. Whatever feels as if it is spinning out of control is in His hands. Be reminded that He is wise, loving, and faithful! Let your anxious thoughts be turned to joy because of God's consolation.

Lord, You are my Father, but You are also my King. You reign and rule over all things. Take my anxiety and turn it into trust. Replace my fear with faith. Console me with Your promises. I know that there is nothing in my life that has not first passed through Your love. Help me rest in that truth today. In Jesus' name, amen.

- Why is anxiety great within you right now?
- What are one or two things you can do today to allow God's love and truth to console you?

Every Friend Needs Encouragement

Encourage one another daily, as long as it is called "Today,"
so that none of you may be hardened by sin's deceitfulness.
—HEBREWS 3:13

When I opened the envelope, I had no idea what was inside. But I love gifts, so just the mention from my friend that she had something for me made my heart swell with anticipation and joy. A beautiful note awaited me, and her kind and thoughtful words provided tremendous encouragement during an especially stressful season. Not to mention she included a gift card to my favorite coffee shop!

Encouragement is a powerful weapon against weariness. It's no wonder that the Bible so often tells us to encourage one another. I love that Hebrews 3:13 tells us to encourage one another "daily." Why? Because we need encouragement every single day. But biblical encouragement is unique in that our kind, thoughtful, and uplifting words are meant to lead someone closer to the Lord. In the Old Testament, Jonathan didn't just encourage or strengthen David; Jonathan helped his friend "find strength in God" (1 Samuel 23:16).

Biblical encouragement can express love, show gratitude, and remind someone of God's promises or truth. Encouragement fills others with the faith to keep going, to persevere in a challenging season. It can come in the form of a handwritten note, a conversation over lunch or coffee, a quick text, or a card like the one I received. Whatever form it takes, encouragement is sure to fill a friend who is running on empty.

When is the last time you encouraged someone? Have you recently texted a friend, written a note, or sent a message to affirm her as a mom? Don't let another day go by—today, right now—let someone know you are thinking of her and how grateful you are for her!

Father, thank You for the gift of friendship. Show me today which of my friends needs to be encouraged. Help me be aware of people in my life who are running on empty or feeling discouraged or alone. Let my words be a simple way to give them strength and joy in this season. In Jesus' name, amen.

- When has the encouragement of another friend or family member filled you with strength and joy?
- Who is one person you can encourage today?

Open Your Home and Your Heart

Offer hospitality to one another without grumbling.

—1 PETER 4:9

One of my favorite things about the city we live in is the food. We have cuisine from all over the world. Eating out and trying new food is something we do often. But I also enjoy having people in our home. We love to open our home and share our favorite foods—and our hearts—with people we love.

Have you ever noticed that Jesus seemed to love food too? How often He broke bread with someone? He frequently went to someone's home, shared a meal or a drink with people, and engaged them in conversation. Jesus gave us great examples of how God can use the ordinary act of eating together to make a difference in the world.

Jesus ate with tax collectors at the home of Levi (Luke 5:27–31). He shared a meal in the home of Mary and Martha (Luke 10:38–42). He even invited Himself over to Zacchaeus's house for dinner (Luke 19:1–10)! For Jesus, sharing a meal was a key opportunity for mission to happen in

God's kingdom. Over and over again we see Him loving and serving those around Him through the act of hospitality.

Think about that for a moment. We can live on mission, have an impact on the world, right from home. Throughout the Bible, hospitality was seen as a primary way for Christians to open their hearts to others. Following their example, we can open our homes not to impress others, but to serve them.

As we open our homes and our hearts to neighbors, friends, or coworkers, God may use us to help them open their hearts to Jesus. This ordinary act can allow God to do extraordinary things!

Father, help me be willing to open my home to love and serve other people. Give me the peace and reassurance that my home doesn't have to be perfect in order for Your presence to be felt by others. Please use the simple, ordinary act of sharing a meal to make an extraordinary difference in the lives of those who join us. In Jesus' name, amen.

- Why is it important to remember that hospitality is not for impressing people, but for serving them?
- In what ways does hospitality provide a great opportunity to love and serve someone else?

Discipline, Not Punishment

No discipline seems pleasant at the time, but painful.
Later on, however, it produces a harvest of righteousness
and peace for those who have been trained by it.
—HEBREWS 12:11

What do you think of when you hear the word *discipline*? For a lot of people, the word discipline evokes memories of being grounded for two weeks, getting sent to your room, or worse yet, spankings. Whatever you think of, it's usually not good!

Maybe that's because when we hear the word, we generally think of being punished instead of teaching and training. There is a big difference between the two. Being punished focuses on penalizing a child. A child does something wrong and is immediately scolded, lectured, or dealt a series of consequences. Such punishment is designed to change a child's behavior. But biblically, discipline is far more than just penalizing a child.

Discipline is designed to be carried out in a loving relationship. While there are still consequences for the child, discipline focuses more on corrective teaching and training. It might feel painful at the time, but in the long run, biblical discipline sets up our kids for growth and maturity in the years to come. When we slow down, are patient, teach, instruct, and hold our kids accountable, we are doing far more for them than penalizing them for bad behavior. We are helping to shape their hearts.

When God created the family, He gave us as parents the authority and privilege of loving and leading our children toward a growing relationship with Christ. Ask God daily to help you train and teach your child, focusing on loving and godly discipline rather than on punishment.

Father, Your Word says that You discipline me out of Your love for me. You lovingly teach me, train me, and correct me in order to grow me. Help me not to parent out of anger or frustration. Give me Your heart for my kids. Teach me to be a mom who disciplines by lovingly correcting and instructing them toward a relationship with You. In Jesus' name, amen.

- Do you tend to punish or discipline? What are the differences between the two?
- What can help you focus more on discipline instead of punishment?

Choosing Wisely

Jonah ran away from the LORD and headed
for Tarshish . . . to flee from the LORD.
—JONAH 1:3

I've run from God a time or two. Fortunately, I have yet to be swallowed by a fish. Jonah is one guy who wasn't so fortunate! If you've ever read the Old Testament book of Jonah, then you are familiar with his story.

God told Jonah to go to Nineveh and preach there. He wanted Jonah to call the people of that city to turn away from their sins and turn to God. Instead of heading to Nineveh, though, Jonah decided "to flee from the LORD" (Jonah 1:3). He got on a boat and sailed for Tarshish, a city in the opposite direction from Nineveh. Along the way, Jonah was thrown from the boat and swallowed by a large fish. Not exactly what Jonah was expecting when he walked through the "open door" of that boat sailing for Tarshish!

Jonah's story is a good reminder for us that not all open doors are opened by God. God could have easily closed the door to Tarshish, making it impossible for Jonah to run, but He didn't. He allowed Jonah to choose. Jonah saw two options: Nineveh or Tarshish. And he picked the wrong one. Jonah quickly found out that not every open door is God's calling. Sometimes those open doors are actually opportunities to run from God instead of toward God.

Are you wrestling with a difficult decision? Are you praying about a new direction at work or in life? Remember the story of Jonah. Not every opportunity that comes our way is necessarily from God. We need to pray. Search God's Word. Receive godly counsel from friends and family. Then we can choose wisely, remembering that in life, we'll have many opportunities that aren't God's calling.

Father, You alone are the one who directs my steps. You are faithful, even when I am unfaithful. Give me wisdom to keep in step with You. Show me clearly when to say no to opportunities and when to say yes. In Jesus' name, amen.

- When have you stepped through an open door that you discovered wasn't the right decision? In what ways did God use that season or those circumstances to grow you?
- How do you discern when something is an open door but not God's calling?

Finding Joy in Letting Go

At that time Jesus, full of joy through the Holy Spirit,
said, "I praise you, Father, Lord of heaven and earth,
because you have hidden these things from the wise
and learned, and revealed them to little children."

—LUKE 10:21

*E*very time I drop off our oldest son at work, I feel a twinge of emotion in my heart. He just turned fifteen, got his driver's permit, and started his first job. My little boy isn't so little anymore. He is becoming a young man.

Have you felt that feeling I'm talking about? That feeling that reminds you your kids aren't going to be kids forever? One of the things God wants to do in us is give us joy—not just in raising our kids, but also in letting our kids go. Even Jesus found joy in letting go.

Several years ago a pastor friend asked my husband and me, "Do you know where the Bible says Jesus was full of joy?" *Wasn't He always full of joy?* I wondered. While Jesus was indeed joyful, the Bible tells us of a specific time when Jesus was "full of joy."

We read in Luke 10 that Jesus was "full of joy" after He had sent out

His disciples. Having taught them and modeled ministry for them, He sent them out to do what He had raised them to do. And we're told, He was "full of joy."

As a mom, I'm reminded that there can be great joy in letting our kids go. We brought them into the world. We are bringing them up in the knowledge of God and His Word. But ultimately our calling is to release them into the world to live for God's glory. I find joy when I focus on what they will gain and not what I will lose.

Father, thank You for never letting my kids go. I know that even when my kids leave my home, they will never truly be out of Your heart or hands. Give me joy in not only raising them, but in releasing them as well. In Jesus' name, amen.

- In what ways can it be selfish for a mom to not want to let her kids go?
- How does Jesus' example help you let go of your kids with joy?

....

....

....

....

....

....

....

....

....

....

Notes

1. R. Laird Harris, Gleans L. Archer Jr., and Bruce K. Waltke, *Theological Wordbook of the Old Testament* (Chicago: Moody Publishers, 1980), 45–46.
2. Thomas à Kempis, *The Imitation of Christ: A Timeless Classic for Contemporary Readers*, trans. William C. Creasy (Notre Dame: Ave Maria Press, 2017), 70.
3. Rick Warren, *The Purpose-Driven Life* (Grand Rapids: Zondervan, 2002), 148.
4. Henri J.M. Nouwen, *The Inner Voice of Love: A Journey Through Anguish to Freedom*, (New York: Crown Publishing Group, 2010), 25.